THE
FRENCH REVOLUTION

D1871615

THE FRENCH REVOLUTION

A SHORT HISTORY

BY

R. M. Johnston

GYAN

Published by

Gyan Publishing House
5, Ansari Road
Daryaganj, New Delhi-110002
Phone: 011-47034999, 9811692060
E-mail: books@gyanbooks.com

Distribution Network
gyanbooks.com
India, USA, Canada, UK, Australia, France

© Publisher
All rights reserved. No part of this work may be reproduced, stored, adapted, or transmitted in any form or by any means, electronic, mechanical, photocopying, micro-filming, recording or otherwise, or translated in any language, without the prior written permission of the copyright owner and the publisher.

ISBN : 978-81-212-6426-6 (PB)
First Published, 1910

2nd Impression 2022

Printed at: Gyan Press, Delhi.

The book is sold subject to the condition that it shall not, by way of trade or otherwise, be lent, resold, hired out, or otherwise circulated without the prior publisher's written consent.

THE FRENCH REVOLUTION
Author: R. M. JOHNSTON

1. Voltaire. 2. Marie Antoinette on her way to the guillotine. 3. Fouquier-Tinville. 4. Carrier. 5. Danton before the Tribunal Révolutionnaire.

The French Revolution

A SHORT HISTORY

By

R. M. Johnston

1910.

TO

Rayner Neate

IN MEMORY OF OLD PEMBROKE DAYS

PREFACE

The object of this book is similar to that with which, a few years ago, I wrote a short biography of Napoleon. The main outlines of the Revolution, the proportion and relation of things, tend to become obscured under the accumulation of historical detail that is now proceeding. This is an attempt, therefore, to disentangle from the mass of details the shape, the movement, the significance of this great historical cataclysm. To keep the outline clear I have deliberately avoided mentioning the names of many subordinate actors; thinking that if nothing essential was connected with them the mention of their names would only tend to confuse matters. Similarly with incidents, I have omitted a few, such as the troubles at Avignon, and changed the emphasis on others, judging freely their importance and not following the footsteps of my predecessors, as in the case of the capture of the Bastille, the importance of which was vastly exaggerated by early writers on the subject.

The end of the Revolution I place at Brumaire,—as good a date as any, though like all others, open to criticism. The present narrative, however, will be found to merge into that of my *Napoleon,* which forms its natural continuation after that date.

CAMBRIDGE, MASS., Feb., 1909.

CONTENTS

CONTENTS

THE FRENCH REVOLUTION

CHAPTER I

THE PERSPECTIVE OF THE FRENCH REVOLUTION

THE magnitude of an event is too apt to lie with its reporter, and the reporter often fails in his sense of historical proportion. The nearer he is to the event the more authority he has as a witness, but the less authority as a judge. It is time alone can establish the relation and harmony of things. This is notably the case with the greatest event of modern European history, the French Revolution, and the first task of the historian writing a century later, is to attempt to catch its perspective. To do this the simplest course will be to see how the Revolution has been interpreted from the moment of its close to the present day.

It was Madame de Staël, under the influence of Constant, who first made Europe listen to reason after the Bourbon restoration of 1815.

Her *Considérations sur la Révolution francaise*, published in 1818, one year after her death, was a bold though temperate plea for the cause of political liberty. At a moment of reaction when the Holy Alliance proclaimed the fraternity not of men but of monarchs, and the direct delegation by Divine Providence of its essential virtues to Alexander, Frederick William and Francis,—at a moment when the men of the Convention were proscribed as regicides, when the word Jacobin sent a thrill of horror down every respectable spinal chord, the daughter of Necker raised her voice to say that if, during the stormy years just passed, the people of France had done nothing but stumble from crime to folly and from folly to crime, the fault did not, after all, lie with them, but with the old régime. If Frenchmen had failed to show the virtues of freemen, it was because they had for so many centuries been treated as slaves. This was in 1818, three years after Waterloo.

Madame de Staël was a pamphleteer; the historians soon followed. Thiers in 1823, Mignet in 1824, produced the first important histories of the Revolution; the former more eloquent, more popular; the latter more ballasted with documentary evidence, more accurate, more pedestrian, in fact, to this day, in its negative manner, one of the best general histories of the matter. Both of these writers were too near their subject and too hampered by the reactionary surroundings of the moment to be successful when dealing with the larger questions the French Revolution involved. Thiers, going a step beyond Madame de Staël, fastened eagerly on the heroic aspects of his subject. It was with this emphasis that later, under the more liberal régime of Louis Philippe, he continued his work through the epoch of Napoleon and produced his immensely popular but extremely unsound history of the Consulate and the Empire. In 1840 the remains of Napoleon were transferred from St. Helena to Paris, and were processionally drawn to the Invalides surrounded by the striking figures and uniforms of a handful of surviving veterans, acclaimed by the ringing rhetoric of Victor Hugo, who in prose and in verse vividly formulated the Napoleonic legend. And just before and just after this event, so made to strike the imagination and to prepare changes of opinion, came a series of notable books. They were all similar in that they bore the stamp of the romanticism of the thirties and forties, interpreting history in terms of the individual; but they differed in their political bias. These works were written by Carlyle, Louis Blanc, Lamartine and Michelet.

Carlyle's French Revolution belongs far more to the domain of literature than to that of history. Its brilliancy may still dazzle those who are able to think of Carlyle as no more than the literary artist; it will not blind those who see foremost in him the great humanitarian. He was too impulsive an artist to resist the high lights of his subject, and was hypnotized by Versailles and the guillotine just as his contemporary Turner was by the glories of flaming sunsets and tumbling waves. The book is a magnificent quest for an unfindable hero, but it is not the French Revolution.

Carlyle's French contemporaries add the note of the party man to his individualistic impressionism, and all three are strong apologists of the Revolution. Lamartine extols the Girondins; Blanc sanctifies Robespierre, whom he mistakes for an apostle of socialism; Michelet, as enthusiastic as either, but larger in his views and much more profound as a scholar, sees the Revolution as a whole and hails in it the regeneration of humanity. Within a few days of the publication of his first volumes, France had risen in revolution once more and had proclaimed the Second Republic. She then, in the space of a few months, passed through all the phases of political thought which Thiers, Blanc, Lamartine and Michelet had glorified—the democratic, the bourgeois, the autocratic republic, and finally the relapse into the empire—the empire of Louis Napoleon.

And, essentially, the histories of the Revolution produced by these writers were special pleadings for a defeated cause, springing up in the year 1848 to a new assertion. Under the Second Empire, with autocracy even more triumphant than under the brothers of Louis XVI, they became the gospels of the recalcitrant liberalism of France; Michelet the gospel of the intellectuals, Blanc the gospel of the proletarians. De Tocqueville added his voice to theirs, his *Ancien Régime* appearing in 1856. Then came 1870, the fall of the Empire, and 1871, the struggle between the middle class republic of Thiers, and the proletarian republic of Paris. The latter, vanquished once more, disappeared in a nightmare of assassination and incendiarism.

It was under the impression of this disaster that Taine set to work to investigate the past of his country, and particularly the great Revolution on which all else appeared to be founded. Between 1875 and 1894 he produced his *Origines de la France Contemporaine,* which in a sense supplanted all previous works on the Revolution. Behind it could be plainly perceived a huge scaffolding of erudite labour, and the working of an intellect of abnormal power; but what was not so apparent, and is now only being slowly recognised, was that much of this erudition was hasty and inspired by preconceived opinions, and that Taine's genius was more philosophic than historic. Assuming the validity of the impressions he had formed when witnessing the agony of Paris in the spring of 1871, his history of the Revolution was a powerful and brilliant vindication of those impressions. But it is only the philosopher who forms his opinions before considering the facts, the historian instinctively reverses the order of these phenomena. As it was, Taine's great work made a tremendous impact on the intellect of his generation, and nearly all that has been written on the Revolution since his day is marked with his mark. His thesis was that the Church and the State were the great institutions whereby brute man had acquired his small share of justice and reason, and that to hack at the root of both State and Church was fatal; it could only lead to the dictatorship of the soldier or to that of the mob. Of these two evils the former appeared to him the less, while the latter he could only think of in terms of folly and outrage. Taine's conservatism was the reaction of opinion against the violence of the Commune and the weak beginnings of the Third Republic, as Michelet's liberalism had been its reaction against Orleanist and Bonapartist middle class and military dictation.

Since Taine's great book, the influence of which is, in this year 1909, only just beginning to fade, what have we had? Passing over von Sybel's considerable and popular history of the Revolution, we have Sorel's *L' Europe et la Révolution française,* more historical, more balanced than Taine's work, clear in style and in arrangement, but on the whole superficial in ideas and incorrect in details. Of far deeper significance is the *Histoire Socialiste* of Jean Jaurès, of which the title is too narrow; *Histoire du peuple,* or *Histoire des classes ouvrières,* would have more closely defined the scope of this remarkable work. Here we have a new phenomenon, history written for the labouring class and from the point of view of the labouring class. And although not free from the taint of the party pamphlet, not of the first rank for historical erudition, intellectual force or artistic composition, Jaurès' history presents the Revolution under the aspect that gives most food for thought and that places it most directly in touch with the problems of the present.

Last of all, what of the labours of the professed historian of to-day? Few of the writers just named could stand the tests rigidly applied to the young men sent out in large numbers of recent years by the universities as technically trained historians. Of these many have turned their attention to the vast field offered by the Revolution and some have done good work. The trend of modern effort, however, is to straighten out the details but to avoid the large issues; to establish beyond question the precise shade of the colour of Robespierre's breeches, but to give up as unattainable having any opinion whatever on the French Revolution as a whole. Not but that, here and there, excellent work is being done. Aulard has published an important history of the Revolution which is a good corrective to Taine's; the Ministry of Public Instruction helps the publication of the documents drawn up to guide the States-General, a vast undertaking that sheds a flood of light on the economic condition of France in 1789. The historians have, in fact, reached a moment of more impartiality, more detachment, more strict setting out of facts; and with the general result that the specialist benefits and the public loses.

What has been said should explain why it is that the Revolution appears even more difficult to treat as a whole at the present day than it did at the time of Thiers and Mignet. The event was so great, the shock was so severe, that from that day to this France has continued to reel and rock from the blow. It is only within the most recent years that we can see going on under our eyes the last oscillations, the slow attainment of the new democratic equilibrium. The end is not yet, but what that end must eventually be now seems clear beyond a doubt. The gradual political education and coming to power of the masses is a process that is the logical outcome of the Revolution; and the joining of hands of a wing of the intellectuals with the most radical section of the working men, is a sign of our times not lightly to be passed over. From Voltaire before the Revolution to Anatole France, at the present day, the tradition and development is continuous and logical.

It now remains to be said that if this is the line along which the perspective of the Revolution is to be sought, this is not the place in which the details of that perspective can be adequately set out. That must be reserved for a history of far larger dimensions, and of much slower achievement, of which a number of pages are already written. In this volume nothing more can be attempted than a sketch in brief form, affording a general view of the Revolution down to the year 1799, when Bonaparte seized power.

CHAPTER II

VERSAILLES

AT the close of the 18th century France had more nearly reached her growth than any of her great European rivals; she was far more like the France of to-day, than might at first be supposed by an Englishman, American or German, thinking of what his own country accomplished during the 19th century. Her population of about 25,000,000 was three times more numerous than that of England. Paris, with 600,000 inhabitants or more, was much nearer the present-day city in size than any other capital of Europe, except Naples. Socially, economically, politically, notwithstanding gross abuses, there was great development; and the reformer who remodelled the institutions of France in 1800 declared that the administrative machine erected by the Bourbons was the best yet devised by human ingenuity. Large manufacturing cities and a number of active ports indicated the advent of a great economic period.

All this reposed, however, on a very incongruous foundation. Feudalism, mediævalism, autocracy, had built up a structure of caste distinction and class privilege to which custom, age, stagnation and ignorance, lent an air of preordained and indispensable stability. The Church, most privileged of all corporations, turned her miracles and her terrors, both present and future, into the most powerful buttress of the fabric. The noblesse, supreme as a caste, almost divided influence with the Church. The two, hand in hand, dominated France outside the larger towns. Each village had its curé and its seigneur. The curé collected his tithes and inculcated the precepts of religion, precepts which at the close of the 18th century, preached Bourbonism as one of the essential manifestations of Providence on earth. The seigneur, generally owning the greater part of all freehold property, not only weighed as a landlord but exercised many exclusive privileges, and applied the most drastic of sanctions to the whole as the local administrator of justice. There were hundreds of devout priests and of humane seigneurs, but a proportion, conspicuous if small, were otherwise; and the system gave such an opportunity for evil doing, that opinion naturally, but unjustly, converted the ill deeds of the few into the characteristic of the whole class.

The culmination of this system, its visible and emphatic symbol, fastened on Paris like a great bloated tumour eating into the heart of France, was Versailles. But compared with class privilege, the Church, and the seigneur, Versailles was a recent phenomenon, invented by Louis XIV little more than one hundred years before the outbreak of the Revolution. At the beginning of the 17th century the French monarchy had somewhat suddenly emerged from the wars of religion immensely strengthened. Able statesmen, Henry IV, Sully, Richelieu, Mazarin, Louis XIV, had brought it out of its struggle with the feudal aristocracy triumphant. Before the wars of religion began the French noble was still mediæval in that he belonged to a caste of military specialists and that his provincial castle was both his residence and his stronghold. The struggle itself was maintained largely by his efforts, by the military and political power of great nobles, Guises, Montmorencys and others. But when the struggle closes, both religion, its cause, and the great noble its supporter, sink somewhat into the background, while the king, the kingly power, fills the eye. And the new divine right monarchy, triumphant over the feudal soldier and gladly accepted as the restorer of order by the middle class, sets to work to consolidate this success; the result is Versailles.

The spectacular palace built by Louis XIV threw glamour and prestige about the triumphant monarchy. It drew the great nobles from their castles and peasantry, and converted them into courtiers, functionaries and office holders. To catch a ray of royal favour was to secure the gilt edging of distinction, and so even the literature, the theology, the intellect of France, quickly learned to revolve about the dazzling Sun King of Versailles, Louis XIV.

Versailles could not, however, long retain such elements of vitality as it possessed. It rapidly accomplished its work on the feudal aristocracy, but only at a great price. With Louis XIV gone, it began to crumble from corruption within, from criticism without. Louis XV converted the palace into the most gorgeous of brothels, and its inmates into the most contemptible and degraded of harlots and pimps. The policy of France, still royal under Louis XIV, was marked by the greed, lewdness and incapacity of Richelieu and Dubois, of Pompadour and du Barry. When the effluvious corpse of Louis XV was hastily smuggled from Versailles to the Cathedral of St. Denis in 1774, that seemed to mark the final dissolution into rottenness of the Bourbon-Versailles régime. That régime already stank in the nostrils of public opinion, a new force which for half a century past had been making rapid progress in France.

The great religious and military struggle of the 16th and 17th centuries had in one direction resulted in enhancing the prestige and crystallizing the power of the French monarchy. In another direction it had resulted in establishing even more firmly the new intellectual position of Europe, the spirit of enquiry, of criticism, of freedom of thought. The Roman or supreme doctrine of authority had been questioned, and questioned successfully. It could not be long before the doctrine of Bourbon authority must also be questioned. Even if French thought and literature did for a moment pay tribute at the throne of Louis XIV the closing years of the century were marked by the names of Leibnitz, Bayle and Newton; the mercurial intelligence of France could not long remain stagnant with such forces as these casting their influence over European civilization.

The new century was not long in, the Regent Philip of Orléans had not long been in power, before France showed that Versailles had ceased to control her literature. A new Rabelais with an 18th century lisp, Montesquieu, by seasoning his *Lettres Persanes* with a sauce piquante compounded of indecency and style, succeeded in making the public swallow some incendiary morsels. The King of France, he declared, drew his power from the vanity of his subjects, while the Pope was "an old idol to whom incense is offered from sheer habit"; nothing stronger has been said to this day. A few years later, in his *Esprit des Lois,* he produced a work of European reputation which eventually proved one of the main channels for the conveyance of English constitutional ideas to the thinking classes of France

An even greater influence than Montesquieu was Voltaire. He exercised an irresistible fascination on the intellectual class by the unrivalled lucidity and logic of his powerful yet witty prose. He carried common sense to the point of genius, threw the glamour of intellect over the materialism of his century, and always seized his pen most eagerly when a question of humanity and liberalism was at stake. He had weak sides, was materialistic in living as in thinking, and had nothing of the martyr in his composition; yet, after his fashion, he battled against obscurantism with all the zeal of a reformer. He was, in fact, the successor of Calvin. But since Calvin's day Protestantism had been almost extirpated in France, so that the gradual growth of the spirit of enquiry, still proceeding below the surface, had brought it to a point beyond Protestantism. It was atheism that Voltaire stood for, and with the vast majority of the people of France from that day to this the alternative lay between rigid Catholicism on one hand and rigid atheism on the other. The innumerable shades of transition between these extremes, in which English and German Protestantism opened a pioneer track, remained a sealed book for them. In his *Letters on the English,* published in 1734, Voltaire dwells less on constitutional than on religious questions. Liberty of conscience is what he struggles for, and he discerns not only that it is more prudent to attack the Church than the State but that it is more essential; religion is at the root of the monarchical system even if the 18th century ruler is apt to forget it. And the Church gives Voltaire ample opportunity for attack. The bishops and court abbés are often enough sceptics and libertines, though every once in a while they turn and deal a furious blow to maintain the prestige and discipline of their ancient corporation. And when, for a few blasphemous words, they send a boy like the Chevalier de La Barre to the scaffold, to be mutilated and killed, Voltaire's voice rings out with the full reverberation of outraged humanity and civilization: *Ecrasez l' infâme!* He believed that the Revolution, which he like so many others foresaw, would begin by an attack on the priests. It was the natural error of a thinker, a man of letters, concerned more with ideas than facts, with theology than economics.

Above all things, Voltaire stood out as a realist, in the modern sense of the word, and if he detested the Church it was largely because it represented untruth. He did not deflect opinion to the same extent as his great contemporary Rousseau, but he represented it more; and of the men of the Revolution, it was Robespierre, who reigned less than four months, who stood for Rousseau, while Bonaparte, who reigned fourteen years, was the true Voltairian.

Just at the side of Voltaire stood the Encyclopedists, led by Diderot and d'Alembert. The great work of reference which they issued penetrated into every intellectual circle, not only of France but of Europe, and brought with it the doctrines of materialism and atheism. However much they might be saturated with the ideas of Church and State in the Roman-Bourbon form, many of its readers became unconsciously shaken in their fundamental beliefs, and ready to question, to criticize and, when the edifice began to tremble, to accept the Revolution and the doctrine of the rights of the common man.

Voltaire, Diderot, d'Alembert, were at heart essentially aristocrats; for them the common man was an untrustworthy brute of low instincts, and their revolution would have meant the displacement of an aristocracy of the sword by an aristocracy of the intellect. Rousseau stood for the opposite view. To him it was only despotism that degraded man. Remove the evil conditions and the common man would quickly display his inherent goodness and amiability; tenderness to our fellows, or fraternity, was therefore the distinctive trait of manhood. The irrepressible exuberance of Rousseau's kindliness overflowed from his novels and essays into a great stream of fashionable sensibility. During the years of terrific stress that followed, during the butcheries of the guillotine and of the Grande Armée, it was the vogue to be soft-hearted, and even such a fire eater as Murat would pour libations of tears over his friends' waistcoats at the slightest provocation. In his *Contrat Social* Rousseau postulated the essential equality of the governor and the governed. But his sentimental attitude towards man involved a corresponding one towards the Deity; unable to accept Catholicism or even Christianity, he sought refuge from atheism in the arms of the *Etre Suprême.* It was this Supreme Being of Rousseau that was to become the official deity of France during the last days of the Reign of Terror.

An influence of a slightly different sort to that exercised by these writers was that of the theatre. The century had seen the rise of the middle-class man, and his attempts at self expression. The coffee-house and the Freemason's lodge gave facilities for conversation, discussion, opinion; and the increasing number of gazettes supplied these circles with information as to the course of political events. But the gazettes themselves might not venture into the danger-marked field of opinion, and for the fast growing public, especially in the city of Paris, there was no opportunity for comment or criticism on the events of the day. In a tentative way the theatre proved itself a possible medium. In 1730, Voltaire produced his tragedy *Brutus*. It fell flat because of the lines

> . . . et je porte en mon cœur
> La liberté gravée et les rois en horreur.

The audience was too loyal to Bourbonism to accept these sentiments; there were loud murmurs; and *Brutus* had to be withdrawn. As late as 1766, a play on the subject of William Tell was given to an empty house; no one would go to see a republican hero. But from the sixties matters changed rapidly. Audiences show great enthusiasm over rivalries of art, of actors, of authors, of opinions, and every once in a while applaud or boo a sentiment that touches the sacred foundations of the social and political order. At last an author appears on the scene, keen, witty, unscrupulous, resourceful, to seize on this growing mood of the public and to play on it for his own glory and profit.

Beaumarchais, Mirabeau, Dumouriez, Bonaparte, these are the types of the adventurers of the Revolution, and the first only belongs to the period of incubation and also to the domain of letters. Thrown into the war of American independence by his double vocation of secret diplomatic agent and speculator in war supplies, he had espoused the cause of the American people with an enthusiasm that always blazed most brightly when a personal interest was at stake. His enthusiasm for American liberty was easily converted into enthusiasm for the liberty of his own class, and to vindicate that, he put Figaro on the stage.

The first public performance of the *Noces de Figaro,* in 1784, was the culmination of a three years' struggle. Louis XVI had declared the play subversive, and the author had raised a storm of protest in its behalf. A special performance was conceded for the Court; and the Parisian public, irritated at being thus excluded, then raised for the first time the cry of tyranny and oppression. When at last the Government in its weakness made the final concession, and permitted a public performance, the demand for seats was greater than had ever previously been known. The theatre was packed. Great lords and ladies sat elbow to elbow with bourgeois and fashionable women; and when Figaro came on and declaimed against social injustice, the opposite parties in the house stormed approval or disfavour. Figaro is Beaumarchais, is the lower or middle class man, with nothing but his wits with which to force his way through the barriers which privilege has erected across every path along which he attempts to advance. As the valet of Count Almaviva he has seen the man of privilege at close quarters and has sounded his rottenness and incapacity. Because you are a grand seigneur, he says, you think yourself a great genius; but, Monsieur le Comte, to what do you really owe your great privileges? To having put yourself to the inconvenience of being born, nothing more. I, with all my ability and force, I who can work for myself, for others, for my country, I am driven away from every occupation.

That was what the pushing adventurer and witty dramatist had to say, but all through the country thousands of plain, inconspicuous men, doctors, lawyers, merchants, farmers, even here and there a peasant or a noble, the best representatives of the deep-rooted civilization of France, of her keen intelligence, of her uprightness, of her humanity, revolted inwardly at the ineptitude and injustice of her government. As they saw it, the whole system seemed to revolve about Versailles, the abode of the Bourbon King, the happy hunting ground of the privileged courtier, the glittering abode of vice and debauchery, the sink through which countless millions were constantly drained while the poor starved, the badge of dishonour and incapacity which had too frequently been attached to the conduct of France both in war and in peace. The twenty-five millions without the gates gazed at the hundred thousand within, and the more they gazed the louder and more bitter became their comment, the dimmer and the more tawdry did the glitter of it all appear to them, and the weaker and more half-hearted became the attitude of the one hundred thousand as they attempted by insolence and superciliousness to maintain the pose of their inherited superiority.

CHAPTER III

ECONOMIC CRISIS

EVEN under such conditions the Bourbon monarchy might have survived much longer had it not failed badly at one specific point. Napoleon himself declared that it was in its financial management that the *ancien régime* had broken down; and although for a long period historians chose to accentuate the political and social aspects of the Revolution, of recent years the economic has been the point of emphasis. And it was to consider a financial problem that the States-General were summoned in 1789; while most of the riots that broke out in Paris that same year were due to scarcity of food.

The editors of the Encyclopædia had not neglected economic questions, and had given much employment to a number of writers who ranked as Economists or as Physiocrats. Among the men most interested in such questions were Quesnay, the physician of Madame de Pompadour; Turgot, the ablest minister of

Louis XVI, and the Marquis de Mirabeau, father of a more famous son. They concerned themselves, among other things, with theories of agriculture largely based on the conditions of their country. With her large population France could with difficulty produce sufficient food for her people. The wheat which she did produce was brought to market under extremely bad conditions of distribution and of payment. The century witnessed what appeared to be an endless succession of short crops and consequent famine. Viewing these conditions as a whole, the economic thinkers concluded that the foundations of the State must repose on agriculture, and they quickly voiced a demand that there should be encouragement for the production of wheat and free circulation.

Towards the end of the reign of Louis XV the effect of these economic doctrines began to be felt. Several efforts were made to remove the restrictions on the circulation of wheat. These efforts, however, proved unavailing until after the meeting of the States-General, and that largely because of the powerful interests that were concerned in maintaining the wheat question as it then existed. The conditions were curious and are of great importance in their relation to the outbreak of the Revolution.

Wheat had become the great medium of financial speculation. It was an article that came on the market at a stated period in large quantities, though in quantities which experience showed were rarely sufficient to meet the requirements of the succeeding twelve months. The capitalist who could pay cash for it, and who had the means of storing it, was therefore nearly certain of a moderate profit, and, if famine occurred, of an extravagant one. That capitalist of necessity belonged to the privileged classes. Frequently religious communities embarked in these ventures, and used their commodious buildings as granaries. Syndicates were formed in which all varieties of speculators entered, from the bourgeois shopkeeper of the provincial town to the courtier and even the King. But popular resentment, the bitter cry of the starving, applied the same name to all of them: from Louis XV to the inconspicuous monk they were all *accapareurs de blé,* cornerers of wheat. And their profits rose as did hunger and starvation. The computation has been put forward that in the year 1789 one-half of the population of France had known from experience the meaning of the word hunger; can it be wondered if the curse of a whole people was attached to any man of whom it might be said that he was an *accapareur de blé?*

The privileged person, king or seigneur, bishop or abbot, levied feudal dues along the roads and waterways, so that a boatload of wine proceeding from Provence to Paris was made to pay toll no less than forty times en route. He owned the right of sitting as judge in town or village, and of commanding the armed force that made judgment effective. Where he did not own the freehold of the farm, he held oppressive feudal rights over it, and in the last resort reappeared in official guise as one of an army of officials whose chief duty it was not so much to ensure justice, good government, or local improvement, as to screw more money out of the taxpayer. Chief of all these officials were the King's intendants, working under the authority of the Controleur-Genéral des Finances.

The Controleur was the most important of the King's ministers, and had charge of nearly all the internal administration of the kingdom. He not only collected the revenue, but had gradually subordinated every other function of government to that one. So he took charge of public works, of commerce and of agriculture, and directed the operations of an army of police, judicial and military officials—and all for the more splendid maintenance of Versailles, Trianon, and the courtiers.

In the provinces he was represented by the intendant. This official's duties varied to a certain extent with his district or *généralité*. In administration France showed the transition that was proceeding from feudalism to centralized monarchism. Provinces had been acquired one by one, and many of them still retained local privileges. Of these the chief was that of holding provincial Estates, and where this custom prevailed, the chief duty of the Estates lay in the assessment of taxes. Where the province was not *pays d' état,* it was the intendant who distributed the taxation. He enforced its collection; directed the *maréchaussèe,* or local police; sat in judgment when disorder broke out; levied the militia, and enforced roadmaking by the *corvée.* Thirty intendants ruled France; and the modern system with its prefects is merely a slight modification devised by Napoleon on the great centralizing and administrative scheme of the Bourbon monarchy.

The taxes formed a somewhat complicated

system, but they may, for the present purpose, be grouped as follows: taxes that were farmed; direct taxes; the gabelle; feudal and ecclesiastical taxes.

In 1697 had begun the practice of leasing indirect taxes for the space of six years to contractors, the *fermiers généraux*. They paid in advance, and recouped themselves by grinding the taxpayer to the uttermost. They defrauded the public in such monopolies as that of tobacco, which was grossly adulterated; and they enforced payments not only with harshness and violence, but with complete disregard for the ruin which their exactions entailed. The government increased the yield of the *ferme* in a little less than a century from 37 to 180 millions of livres or francs,[1] and yet the sixty farmers continued to increase in wealth. They formed the most conspicuous group of plutocrats when the Revolution broke out and were among the first victims of popular indignation. Of the direct taxes the most important in every way was the *taille*. It brought in under Louis XVI about 90 millions of francs. It represented historically the fundamental right of the French monarch to tax his

[1] The franc comes into use at the period of the Revolution. It will be employed throughout instead of *livres* as the standard denomination.

subjects delegated to him by the Estates of the kingdom in the 15th century. By virtue of that delegated power it was the Royal Council that settled each year what amount of *taille* should be levied. It was enforced harshly and in such a manner as to discourage land improvement. It was also the badge of social inferiority, for in the course of centuries a large part of the wealthier middle classes had bought or bargained themselves out of the tax, so that to pay it was a certain mark of the lower class or *roture*. *Taillable, roturier,* were terms of social ostracism impatiently borne by thousands.

Other direct taxes were the capitation, bringing in over 50 millions, the *dixiéme,* the *don gratuit*. But more important than any of these was the great Government indirect tax, the monopoly on salt, or *gabelle*. Exemptions of all sorts made the price vary in different parts of France, but in some cases as much as 60 francs was charged for the annual quantity which the individual was assessed at, that same individual as often as not earning less than 5 francs a week. So much smuggling, fraud and resistance to the law did the *gabelle* produce that it took 50,000 officials, police and soldiers, to work it. In the year 1783 no less than 11,000 persons, many of them women and children, were arrested for infraction of the *gabelle* laws.

Last of all, the tithe and feudal dues were added to the burden. The priest was maintained by the land. The seigneur's rights were numerous, and varied in different parts of the country. They bore most heavily in the central and northeastern parts of France, most lightly in the south, where Roman law had prevailed over feudal, and along most of the Atlantic coast line, as in Normandy. These feudal dues will be noticed later in connection with the famous session of the States-General on the 4th of August, 1789.

In all this system of taxation there was only one rule that was of universal application, and that was that the burden should be thrown on the poor man's shoulders. The clergy had compounded with the Crown. The nobles or officials were the assessors, and whether they officiated for the King, for the Provincial Estates or for themselves, they took good care that their own contributions to the royal chest should be even less proportionately than might legally be demanded of them. And after all the money had been driven into the treasury it was but too painfully evident what became of it. The fermiers and the favourites scrambled for the millions and flaunted their splendour in the face of those who paid for it. The extravagance of the Court was equalled only by its ineptitude. No proper accounts were kept, because all but the taxpayers found their interest in squandering. Under Madame de Pompadour the practice arose that orders for money payments signed by the King alone should be paid in cash and not passed through the audit chamber, such as it was. Pensions became a serious drain on the revenue and rapidly grew to over 50 millions a year at the end of the reign of Louis XVI. They were not infrequently granted for ridiculous or scandalous reasons, as in the case of Ducrest, hairdresser to the eldest daughter of the Comtesse d' Artois, who was granted an annual pension of 1,700 francs on her death; the child was then twelve months old; or that of a servant of the actress Clairon, who was brought into the Œuil de Boeuf one morning to tell Louis XV a doubtful story about his mistress; the King laughed so much that he ordered the fellow to be put down for a pension of 600 francs!.

With its finances in such condition the Bourbon monarchy plunged into war with England in 1778, and, for the satisfaction of Yorktown and the independence of the United States, spent 1,500 millions of francs, nearly four years' revenue. At that moment it was estimated that the people of France paid in taxation about 800 millions annually, about one-half of which reached the King's chest. But the burden of debt was so great that by 1789, nearly 250 millions were paid out annually for interest.

To meet this situation the Government tried many men and many measures. There were several partial repudiations of debt. The money was clipped, much to the profit of importers from Amsterdam and other centres of thrift. Necker made way for Calonne, and Calonne for Necker. But these names bring us to the current of events that resulted in the convocation of the States-General by Louis XVI, and that must be made the subject of another chapter.

CHAPTER IV

CONVOCATION OF THE STATES-GENERAL

LOUIS XVI, grandson of Louis XV, came to the throne in 1774. He showed some, but not all, of the characteristics of his family. He was of sluggish intelligence, and extremely slow, not to say embarrassed, in speech. He was heavy in build and in features. His two great interests were locksmithing, which he had learned as a boy, and running the deer and the boar in the great royal forests, St. Germain, Fontainebleau, Rambouillet. He had all the Bourbon *insouciance,* and would break off an important discussion of the Council from indifference, incompetence, or impatience, to go off hunting. Worst of all, for an autocrat, he had not in his nature one particle of those qualities that go to make up the man of action, decision, energy, courage, whole-heartedness. In this he represented the decay of his race, surfeited with power, victim of the system it had struggled so long and so hard to establish. At the best he had flashes of common sense, which, unfortunately for himself, he was never capable of translating into deeds. He was full of good intentions, of a certain underlying honesty and benevolence, all rather obscured by his boorish exterior and manners. Like his ancestors, he ate and drank voraciously, but, unlike them, he did not care for women. He even showed some indifference for his wife at first, but later, when she bore children, he appeared to the public in the character of a good father of the family. In that and some of his other traits he had elements of popularity, and he remained in a way popular almost to the moment of his trial in 1792.

Marie Antoinette of Austria, his wife, was of very different mould; and in her everything made for unpopularity. She had begun under the worst auspices. The French public detested the Austrian alliance into which Madame de Pompadour had dragged France, and had felt the smart of national disgrace during the Seven Years' War, so that a marriage into the Hapsburg-Lorraine family after the conclusion of that war, was very ill received. To make the matter worse a catastrophe marked the wedding ceremonies, and at a great illumination given by the city of Paris, a stampede occurred, in which hundreds of lives were lost. The Austrian princess, *l' Autrichienne,* as she was called from the first, did not mend matters by her conduct. Until misfortune sobered her and brought out her stronger and better side, she was incurably light-headed and frivolous. She was always on the very edge of a *faux pas,* and her enemies did not fail to accuse her of frequent slips beyond the edge. The titled riffraff that had adorned the Louis XV-du Barry court was swept out on the accession of the young Queen, but only to be replaced by a new clique as greedy as the old, and not vastly more edifying. Richelieu and d' Aiguillon only made way for Lauzun, the Polignacs, and Vaudreuil. And if it was an improvement to have a high-born queen rule Versailles instead of a low-born courtesan, the difference was not great in the matter of outward dignity, and especially of the expenditure of public money. Millions that cannot be computed for lack of proper accounts were poured out for the Queen's amusements and for the Queen's favourites, men and women.

It was the Controleur whose function was to fill the Court's bottomless purse. Under this strain and that of the American war, a man of humble origin but of good repute as an economist and accountant was called to the office, the Geneva banker, Jacques Necker. For three years he attempted to carry the burden of the war by small economies effected at many points, which produced the minimum of result with the maximum of friction. Finally, in 1781, the Queen drove him from office. Necker himself provided the excuse by the publication of his *Compte rendu,* a pamphlet which first put the financial crisis fairly before the public.

All that the public knew up to this time was that while the Court maintained its splendour and extravagance, the economic and financial situation was rapidly getting worse. There was no systematic audit, there was no budget, there was no annual account published, so that the finances remained a sealed book, a private matter concerning the King of France only. But here, in Necker's pamphlet, was an account of those finances, that revealed to a certain extent the state of affairs, and, which was even more important, that constituted an appeal to the public to judge the King's administration. Louis was furious at his minister's step, and not only dismissed him, but banished him from Paris.

From 1783 to 1787 the finances were in the hands of Calonne, whose management proved decisive and fatal. His dominant idea was that of a courtier,—always to honour any demand made on the treasury by the King or Queen. To do less would be unworthy of a *gentilhomme* and a devoted servant of their Majesties. So Calonne, bowing gracefully, smiling reassuringly, embarked on a fatal course, borrowing where he could, anticipating in one direction, defaulting in another, but always, and somehow, producing the louis necessary to the enjoyment of the present moment. He reached the end of his tether towards the close of 1786.

It was during Calonne's administration that occurred the famous affair of the diamond necklace. It was a vulgar swindle worked on the Cardinal de Rohan by an adventuress, Mme. de La Motte Valois. Trading on his credulity and court ambitions, she persuaded him to purchase a diamond necklace, which the Queen, so he was told, greatly wished but could not afford. Marie Antoinette was personated in a secret interview given to Rohan, and Mme. de La Motte got possession of the diamonds. Presently the jewellers began to press Rohan for payment, and the secret came out. The

King was furious, and sent Rohan to the royal prison of the Bastille, while Mme. de La Motte was handal to into the legal procedure of the Parlement of Paris.

This incident created great excitement, and was much distorted by public report. It left two lasting impressions, one relating to Mme. de La Motte, the other to the Queen. The adventuress was too obvious a scapegoat to be spared. While Rohan was allowed to leave the Bastille after a short imprisonment, the woman was brought to trial, and was sentenced to public whipping and branding. Her execution was carried out in bungling fashion, and at the foot of the steps leading to the law courts, whence Danton's voice was to reverberate so loudly in his struggle with so-called Justice ten years later, a disgraceful scene occurred. The crowd saw La Motte struggling in the hands of the executioners and rolling with them in the gutter, heard her uttering loud shrieks as the branding iron was at last applied to her shoulders. The impression produced by this revolting spectacle was profound, and was heightened by the universal belief that Marie Antoinette was not less guilty in one direction than Madame de La Motte had been in another. The outbreak of slander and of libel against the Queen goes on accumulating from this moment with ever-increasing force until her death, eight years later. A legend comes into existence, becomes blacker and blacker, and culminates in the atrocious accusations made against her by Hébert before the Revolutionary Tribunal; Messalina and Semiramis are rolled into one to supply a fit basis of comparison. And the population of Paris broods over this legend, and when revolution comes, makes of Marie Antoinette the symbol of all that is monstrous, infamous and cruel in the system of the Bourbons; makes of her the marked victim of the vengeance of the people.

Meanwhile Calonne was struggling to keep his head above water, and in the process had come into conflict with the Parlements, or corporations of judges. At last, in 1786, he went to the King, admitted that he had no money, that he could borrow no more, and that the only hope lay in fundamental reform. He proposed, therefore, a number of measures, of which the most important were that money should be raised by a stamp tax, that a land tax should be the foundation of the revenue, and that it should apply to all proprietors, noble, cleric, and of the Third Estate, with no exceptions. There was no chance, however, as matters stood, of persuading the Parlements to register decrees for these purposes, so Calonne proposed that the King should summon an assembly of the notables of France to give their support to these reforms. Here again, although Calonne and Louis did not realize it, was an appeal to public opinion; the monarchy was unconsciously following the lead of the philosophers, of the dramatists, and of Necker.

In January, 1788, the Notables assembled, "to learn the King's intentions," one hundred and fifty of them, mostly nobles and official persons. In February Calonne put his scheme before them, and then discovered, to his great astonishment, that they declined to give him the support, which was all he wanted of them, and that, on the contrary, they wished to discuss his project, and, in fact, held a very adverse opinion of it. In this the Notables were not factious; they merely had enough sense of the gravity of the situation to perceive that a real remedy was needed, and that Calonne's proposal did not supply it. His idea was good enough in the abstract, but in practice there was at least one insurmountable objection, which was that the land tax could not be established until a cadastral survey of France had been undertaken—a complicated and lengthy operation. Very soon Calonne and the Notables had embarked on a contest that gradually became heated, until finally Calonne appealed from the Notables to the public by printing and circulating his proposals. The Notables replied by a protest, and declared that the real reform was economy and that the Controleur should place before them proper accounts. This proved the end of Calonne, his position had long been weak, he now toppled over, and was replaced by Loménie de Brienne, Archbishop of Toulouse.

Loménie was an agreeable courtier, and well liked by the Queen, but he was also a liberal, an encyclopedist, and a member of the Assembly of Notables. He succeeded in getting the approval of that body for a loan of 60,000,000 francs, and then, on the 1st of May, 1787, dissolved it. The new minister had, however, come to the opinion that his predecessor's programme was the only possible one, and as soon as he had got rid of the Notables, his late colleagues, he attempted to get the Parlement of Paris to register the new laws.

The Parlement resisted; and popular discontent became a serious feature of the situation. The Chancellor, Lamoignon, was burnt in effigy by the mob. In July, 1787, the Parlement of Paris demanded that the States-General of the kingdom should be assembled. For a whole year the struggle between the judges and the ministers grew hotter and hotter. The arrest of d' Espréménil, one of the leaders of the Parlement, in May, 1788, led to severe rioting in Paris, and only the energetic use of police and troops saved the situation. Not only did the provincial Parlements support that of Paris in its resistance to the Court, but the provinces themselves began to stir, and finally, a month after d' Espréménil's arrest, a large meeting at Grenoble decided to call together the old Estates of the province, the province of Dauphiné.

This was almost civil war, and threatened to plunge France back into the conditions of two centuries earlier. The Government ordered troops to Grenoble to put down the movement. The commanding general, however, on arriving near the city, found the situation so alarming that he agreed to a compromise, whereby the Estates were to hold a meeting, but not in the capital of the province. Accordingly, at the village of Vizille, on the 21st of July, several hundred persons assembled, representing the three orders, nobility, clergy, and

Third Estate of the province; and of these it had been previously agreed that the Third Estate should be allowed double representation.

The leading figure of the assembly of Vizille was Jean Joseph Mounier. He was a middle class man, a lawyer, upright, intelligent, yet moderate, who felt the need of reform, and who was prepared to labour for it. He inspired all the proceedings at Vizille, and as secretary of the Estates, had the chief part in drawing up its resolutions. These demanded the convocation of the States-General of France, pledged the province to refuse to pay all taxes not voted by the States-General, and called for the abolition of arbitrary imprisonment on the King's order by the warrant known as the *lettre de cachet*.

The effect of the resolutions of the assembly of Vizille through France was immediate. They were simple, direct, and voiced the general feeling; they also indicated that the moment had come for interfering in the chronic mismanagement of affairs. So irresistible was their force that Loménie de Brienne and the King accepted them with hardly a struggle. The minister was now at the end of his borrowing powers and in the month of August his tenure of power came to a close. Before leaving office he suspended payments, and issued a decree convoking the States-General for the 1st of May, 1789. He was succeeded by Necker.

It was unfortunate for the Bourbon monarchy that at this great crisis a king and a minister should have come together, both lacking initiative, both lacking courage, and yet not even sympathetic, but, on the contrary, lacking mutual confidence and refusing one another mutual support. And while Louis lacked executive vigour, so Necker tended always to lose himself in figures, in details, in words, in fine sentiments, and to neglect the essential for the unimportant. He was well intentioned but narrow, and merely followed the current of events. From all parts of France advice and representations reached him as to the conditions under which the States-General should be convoked. Their last meeting had been held as far back as 1614, so that there was naturally much uncertainty on questions of procedure. Partly to clear this, partly to find some support for his own timidity, Necker called the Notables together again. They met in November and helped to settle the conditions under which the elections to the States-General and their convocation should take place.

The old constitutional theory of the States-General was that it was an assembly of the whole French nation, represented by delegates, and divided into three classes. Thus it was tribal in that it comprised every Frenchman within its scope, and feudal in that it formed the caste distinctions, noble, clergy, people. In other words it afforded little ground for comparison with the English Parliament; the point at which it approached it nearest being in the matter of the power to vote the taxation levied by the Crown; but this power the States-General had lost so far back as the 15th century.

This fundamental conception entailed another, which was that the delegates of the nation were not members of a parliament or debating assembly, but were mere mandatories charged by the electors with a specific commission, which was to place certain representations before the King. This meant that in the stage previous to the election of these delegates, the electors should draw up a statement of their complaints and a mandate or instructions for their representatives. This was in fact done, and many thousands of *cahiers,* as they were called, were drawn up all over France, in which the demands of as many individuals, or corporations, or bodies of electors were stated. These were summarized into three cahiers for each province, and eventually into three, one from each order, for all France, and these last three were in due course presented to Louis XVI.

As a source of information on the economic and social condition of a country, the cahiers are the most wonderful collection of documents available for the historian. Many of them have been more or less faithfully published, and at the present day the French government is liberally helping on the work of making them public. But in a work of this scope it is impossible to go at length into the state of affairs which they depict; only the most salient features can be dealt with.

First, then, it must be said that the cahiers present at the same time remarkable uniformity and wide divergence. The agreement lies partly in their general spirit, and partly in the repetition of certain formulas preached throughout the country by eager pamphleteers and budding political leaders. The divergence can be placed under three chief heads: the markedly different character of a great part of the cahiers of the clergy from those of the other two orders; provincial divergence and peculiarities of local customs; demands for the maintenance of local privileges. Of the last class, Marseilles, a port with many commercial and political privileges, affords perhaps the most extreme example. The uniformity is to be seen especially in the general spirit of these complaints to the King. One feels, while reading the *cahiers,* the unanimity of a long-suffering people anxious for a release from intolerable misgovernment,—more than that, anxious to have their institutions modernized, but all in a spirit of complete loyalty and devotion to the King and to all that was wise, and good, and glorious, and beneficent, that he still seemed to represent. The illusion of Bourbonism was at that moment, so far as surface appearances went, practically untouched.

The noblesse and the clergy conducted their elections by means of small meetings and chose their delegates from among themselves. The Tiers Etat elected as its representatives men of the upper middle class and professional class; the lower classes, ignorant and politically untutored, were unrepresented and accepted tutelage with more or less alacrity—more in the provinces, less in Paris. But in addition, a small number of men belonging to the privileged orders sought and obtained mandates from the lower. Sieyès and a few other priests, Mirabeau and a few other nobles, were elected to the States-General by the Third Estate.

Sieyès, of powerful mind, a student of constitutionalism, terse and logical in expression, had made a mark during the electoral period with his pamphlet, *Qu'est ce que le Tiers Etat?* What is the Third Estate? His reply was: It is everything; it has been nothing; it should be something. This was a reasonable and forceful exposition of the views of the twenty-five millions. Mirabeau, of volcanic temperament and morals, with the instinct of a statesman and the conscience of an outlaw, greedy of power as of money, with thundering voice, ready rhetoric, and keen perception, turned from his own order to the people for his mandate. He saw clearly enough from the beginning that reform could not stop at financial changes, but must throw open the government of France to the large class of intelligent citizens with which her developed civilization had endowed her.

The outstanding fact brought out by this infiltration of the noblesse and clergy into the

Third Estate, was clear: the deputies to the States-General, whichever order they belonged to, were nearly all members of the educated middle and upper class of France. Part of the deputies of the noblesse stood for class privilege, and so did a somewhat larger part of those of the clergy. But a great number in both these orders were of the same sentiment as the deputies of the Third Estate. They were intelligent and patriotic Frenchmen, full of the teaching of Voltaire, and Rousseau, and Montesquieu, convinced by their eyes as well as by their intellect that Bourbonism must be reformed for its own sake, for the sake of France, and for the sake of humanity.

CHAPTER V

FRANCE COMES TO VERSAILLES

AT the beginning of May, twelve hundred and fourteen representatives of France reached Versailles. Of these, six hundred and twenty-one, more than half, belonged to the Third Estate, and of the six hundred and twenty-one more than four hundred had some connection with the law, while less than forty belonged to the farming class. Little preparation had been made for them; the King had continued to attend to his hounds and horses, the Queen to her balls and dresses, and Necker to his columns of figures, his hopes, and his illusions. But the arrival of this formidable body of men of trained intellect in the royal city, now that it had occurred, at once caused a certain uneasiness. As they walked about the city in curious groups, it was as though France were surveying the phenomenon of Versailles with critical eye; at the very first occasion the courtiers, feeling this, set to work to teach the deputies of the Third Estate a lesson, to put them in their place.

On the 4th and 5th of May the opening ceremonies took place, processions, mass, a sermon, speeches; and the Court's policy, if such it could be called, was revealed. The powerful engine known as etiquette was brought into play, to indicate to the deputies what position and what influence in the State the King intended they should have. This was perhaps the greatest revelation of the inherent weakness of Bourbonism; the system had, in its decline, become little more than etiquette, and Louis XVI seen hard at work in his shirt-sleeves would have shattered the illusions of centuries. And so, by means of the myriad contrivances of masters of ceremonies and Court heralds the Third Estate was carefully made to feel its social inferiority, its political insignificance.

The Third Estate noted these manifestations of the Court with due sobriety, and met the attack squarely. But while on the part of the Court this way of approaching the great national problem never attained a higher dignity than a policy of pin pricks, with the Third Estate it was at once converted into a constitutional question of fundamental importance. Was the distinction between the three orders to be maintained? was the noble or priest a person of social and political privilege? or were the deputies of all to meet in one assembly and have equal votes? That was the great question, as the Third Estate chose to state it, and, translated into historical terms, it meant no less than the passing of the feudal arrangement of society in separate castes into the new system of what is known at our day as democracy.

Nearly all the cahiers of the Third Estate and many of those of the noblesse, had demanded this measure, and the Third Estate on assembling to verify the mandates of its members immediately called on the other two orders to join it in this proceeding. The struggle over this point continued from the 5th of May to the 9th of June, before any decisive step was taken. But as the days went by, apparently in fruitless debate, there was in reality a constant displacement of influence going on in favor of the Third Estate. In the opening session the statement of affairs made by Necker had left a very poor impression. Since then the ministers had done nothing, save to attempt, by a feeble intervention, to keep the orders apart. And all the time the Third Estate was gradually becoming conscious of its own strength and of the feebleness of the adversary. And so at last, on the 10th of June, Sieyès moved, Mirabeau supporting, that the noblesse and the clergy should be formally summoned to join the Tiers, and that on the 12th, verification of powers for the whole of the States-General should take place.

Accordingly on the 12th, under the presidency of the astronomer Bailly, senior representative of the city of Paris, the Tiers began the verification of the deputies' mandates. On the 13th, three members of the clergy, three country priests, asked admission. They were received amid scenes of the greatest enthusiasm, and within a few days their example proved widely contagious. On the 1 th, a new step was taken, and the deputies, belonging now to a body that was clearly no longer the Tiers Etat, voted themselves a *National Assembly*. This was, in a sense, accomplishing the Revolution.

So rapidly did the Tiers now draw the other parts of the Assembly to itself that on the 19th, the Clergy formally voted for reunion. This brought the growing uneasiness and alarm of the Court to a head. Necker's influence was now on the wane. The King's youngest brother, the Comte d' Artois, at this moment on good terms with the Queen, and Marie Antoinette herself, were for putting an end to the mischief before it went further, and they prevailed. It was decided that the King should intervene, and should break up the States-General into its component parts once more by an exercise of the royal authority.

On the morning of the 20th of June, in a driving rain, the deputies arriving at their hall found the doors closed and workmen in possession. This was the contemptuous manner in which the Court chose to intimate to them that preparations were being made for a royal session which was to take place two days later. Alarmed and indignant, the deputies proceeded to the palace tennis court close by,—the *Jeu de Paume,*—and there heated discussion followed. Sieyès, for once in his career imprudent, proposed that the Assembly should remove to Paris. Mounier, conservative at heart, realizing that this meant civil war, temporized, and carried the Assembly with him by proposing a solemn oath whereby those present would pledge themselves not to separate until they had endowed France with a constitution.

On the 23rd, the royal session was held. A great display of troops and of ceremony was made. The deputies assembled in the hall, and the King's speech was read. It was a carefully prepared document, announcing noteworthy concessions as well as noteworthy reservations, but vitiated by two things: the concessions came just too late; the reservations were not promptly and effectively enforced. The King declared that for two months past the States-General had accomplished nothing save wrangling, that the time had therefore arrived for recalling them to their duties. His royal will was that the distinction between the three orders should be maintained, and after announcing a number of financial and other reforms, he ordered the deputies to separate at once. The King then left the hall supported by his attendants, and by the greater part of the nobles and high clergy. There followed a memorable scene, to understand which it is necessary to go back a little.

On the arrival of the deputies at Versailles, they had at once tended to form themselves into groups, messes, or clubs, for eating, social and political purposes. An association of this kind, the Club Breton, so called from the province of its founders, soon assumed considerable importance. Here the forward men of the assembly met and discussed; and here, filtering through innumerable channels, came the news of the palace, the tittle tattle of Trianon and the Œuil de Bœuf, the decisions of the King's council. At every crisis during the struggle at Versailles, the leaders of the assembly knew beforehand what the King and his ministers thought, and what measures they had decided on. All that was necessary therefore was to concert secretly the step most likely to thwart the royal policy, and by eloquence, by persuasion, by entreaty, to cajole the great floating mass of members to follow the lead of the more active minds. The King's speech on the 23rd of June was no surprise to the assembly, and the leaders were prepared with an effective rejoinder.

So when Louis XVI left the hall after commanding the deputies to disperse, the greater part of them kept their seats, and when Dreux Brézé, Master of Ceremonies, noting this, called on the president to withdraw, Bailly replied that the assembly was in session and could not adjourn without a motion. The discussion between Dreux Brézé and Bailly continuing, Mirabeau turned on the King's representative and in his thundering voice declaimed the famous speech, which he had doubtless prepared the night before. "We are here," he concluded, "by the will of the people, and we will only quit at the point of the bayonet." At this de Brézé withdrew and reported to the King for orders. But Louis had done enough for one day, and the only conclusion he could come to was that if the deputies refused to leave the hall, the best course would be for them to remain there. And there in fact they stayed.

Immediately after this scene Necker sent in his resignation. On the morning of the 24th, this was known in Paris, and produced consternation and a run on the banks. To reassure the public, Necker was immediately reinstated, on the basis that Louis should accept, as now seemed inevitable, the fusion of the orders. On the 25th, a large group of nobles headed by the Duc d' Orléans and the Comte de Clermont Tonnerre joined the assembly, and a week later the Assemblée Nationale was fully constituted, the three orders merged into one.

During the two months through which this great constitutional struggle had lasted, the assembly had had a great moral force behind it, a moral force that was fast tending to become something more. The winter of 1788–89 had been one of the most severe of the century. There had been not only the almost chronic shortage of bread, but weather of extraordinary rigour. In the city of Paris the Seine is reported to have been frozen solid, while the suffering among its inhabitants was unparalleled. As an inevitable consequence of this riots broke out. In January there had been food riots in many parts of France that taxed severely the military resources of the Government. They continued during the electoral period, and were occasionally accompanied by great violence. And when the deputies assembled at Versailles there was behind them a great popular force, already half unloosed, that looked to the States-General for appeasement or for guidance.

The procedure which the Third Estate and National Assembly stumbled into, gave this popular force an opportunity for expressing itself. The public was admitted to the opening session, and it continued to come to those that followed. From the public galleries came the loudest sounds of applause that greeted the patriotic orator. The Parisian public quickly fell into the way of making the journey to Versailles to join in these demonstrations, and soon transferred them from the hall of the assembly to the street outside. Mirabeau, Sieyès, Mounier, and other popular members were constantly receiving ovations—and soon learnt to convert them into political weapons; while members who were suspected of reactionary tendencies, especially the higher clergy, met with hostile receptions. And all this, well known both to Court and assembly, was but a faint echo of the great force rumbling steadily twelve miles away in the city of Paris.

The leaders of the assembly did not scruple to use this pressure of public opinion, of popular violence, for all it was worth. And placed as they were it was not surprising that they should have done so. The deputies were only a small group of men in the great royal city garrisoned with all the traditions of the French royalty and 5,000 sabres and bayonets besides. It was natural that they should seek support then, even if that support meant violence, lawlessness or insurrection.

Thus Paris encouraged the assembly, and the assembly Paris. The ferment in the capital was reaching fever-heat just at the moment that the assembly had won its victory over the orders. The working classes were raging for food, the bankers, capitalists and merchants saw in the States-General the only hope of avoiding bankruptcy, the intellectual and professional class was more agitated than any other. The cafés and pamphlet shops of the

Palais Royal were daily more crowded, more excited. And on the 30th of June the army itself began to show symptoms of following the general movement.

The regiment of French guards was a body of soldiers kept permanently quartered in the capital. The men were, therefore, in closer touch with the population than would be the case in ordinary regiments. Their commanding officer at this moment was not only an aristocrat but a martinet, and he completely failed to keep his regiment in hand. Trouble had long been brewing in the ranks and culminated in mutiny and riot at the close of June. Making the most of the state of Paris many of the mutinous guardsmen took their liberty and refused to return to barracks. Clearly what between the accomplished revolt of the Third Estate, the incipient revolt of Paris, and the open mutiny of the troops, something had to be done.

Necker's return to the Ministry had been imposed on the Court, and although his policy of accepting the fusion of the orders was followed, his influence really amounted to little. The Queen and the Comte d' Artois soon plucked up courage after their first defeat, and took up once more the policy of repression; but as it was now apparently useless to attempt to stem the tide by means of speeches or decrees, they persuaded the King that force was the only means. By using the army he could get rid of Necker, get rid of the National Assembly, and reduce Paris to order.

Accordingly the Marshal de Broglie, a veteran of the Seven Years' War, was put in charge of military matters, and an old Swiss officer, the Baron de Besenval, was placed in immediate command of the troops. Regiments were brought in from various quarters, and by the end of the first week of July the Court's measures were developing so fast, and appeared so dangerous, that the assembly passed a vote asking the King to withdraw the troops and to authorize the formation of a civic guard in Paris. The King's answer, delivered on the 10th, was negative and peremptory; his troops were to be employed to put down disorder.

At this crisis the action of the assembly and of Paris became more definitely concerted. The government of the city had been in the hands of a somewhat antiquated board presided over by a provost of the merchants. It was too much out of touch with the existing movement to have any influence, and felt its impotence so keenly that it would willingly have resigned its power. At the time of the elections to the States-General the Government had broken up Paris into sixty electoral districts for the sake of avoiding the possibility of large meetings. These sections, as they were called, had formed committees, and these committees, towards the middle of June, had been coming together again informally and tending towards permanence. On the 23rd of that month, with disorder growing in the city, they had held a joint meeting at the Hotel de Ville, the town house, and the municipality had given them a permanent room there, hoping that their influence would help keep disorder under.

When, on the 11th, the news reached Paris that Louis had refused the assembly's demand for the withdrawal of the troops, the central committee of the sections took matters into its hands and voted the formation of a civic guard for the city of Paris. On the same day the King, now ready to precipitate the crisis, dismissed and exiled Necker, and called the reactionary Breteuil to power. On the 12th, Paris broke out into open insurrection.

It was Camille Desmoulins who set the torch to the powder. This young lawyer and pamphleteer, a brilliant writer, a generous idealist, almost the only reasoned republican in Paris at that day, was one of the most popular figures in the Palais Royal crowds. On the 12th of July, standing on a café table, he announced the news of the dismissal of Necker, the movement of the troops on Paris, and with passion and eloquence declaimed against the Government and called on all good citizens to take up arms. He headed a great procession from the Palais Royal to the Hotel de Ville.

The move on the Hotel de Ville had for its object to procure arms. The committee of the sections had voted a civic guard, but a civic guard to act required muskets. The troops of Besenval were now pressing in on the city, and had nearly encircled it. In a few hours Paris, always hungry, might be reduced to famine, and the troops might be pouring volleys down the streets. The soldiers of the French guards, siding with the people, were already skirmishing with the Germans of the King's regiments, for the army operating against Paris was more foreign than French, and the Swiss and German regiments were placed at the head of the columns for fear the French soldiers would not fire on the citizens. Royal-Etranger, Reinach, Nassau, Esterhazy, Royal-Allemand, Royal-Cravate, Diesbach, such were some of the names of the regiments sent by Louis XVI to persuade his good people of Paris into submission. No wonder that the crowd shouted when Desmoulins told them that the Germans would sack Paris that night if they did not defend themselves.

On the night of the 12th to the 13th, Paris was in an uproar. Royalist writers tell us that gunshops were plundered by the mob, republican writers that the owners of guns voluntarily distributed them. Besenval, lacking instructions from Broglie, and hesitating at what faced him, had done little or nothing; but Paris intended to be ready for him if he should act on the following day.

On the 13th, the disorder and excitement continued. The committee at the Hotel de Ville took in hand the formation of battalions for each section of the city; while Besenval still remained almost inactive at the gates. On the 14th the insurrection culminated, and won what proved to be a decisive victory.

At the east end of Paris stood the Bastille. It was a mediæval dungeon of formidable aspect, armed with many cannon and dominating the outlet from the populous faubourg St. Antoine to the country beyond—one of the mouths of famishing Paris. It contained a great store of gunpowder and a garrison of about 100 Swiss and veterans. The fortress had an evil reputation as a state prison. Although in July, 1789 its cells were nearly all unoccupied, popular legend would have it that numerous victims of royal despotism, arbitrarily imprisoned, lay within its walls. So it was a symbol of the royal authority within Paris, a threat, or reckoned so, to the faubourg St. Antoine and the free movement of food supplies from the east side of the city, a store of guns and ammunition. For all these reasons the mob, undisturbed by Besenval, turned to attack it.

The first effort was in vain. Although the garrison of the Bastille, except its commander, the Marquis de Launay, was disinclined to fire on the mob, and was so short of provisions that resistance was useless, the attackers succeeded in little more than getting possession of some of the outbuildings of the fortress. The musketry which the Governor directed from the keep proved more than the mob cared to face. But the first wave of attack was soon reinforced by another. From the French regiments of Besenval's army a steady stream of deserters was now setting into Paris through every gate. A number of these soldiers and of the men of the regiment of the French guards were drawn to the Bastille by the sound of the firing and now took up the attack with system and vigour. Elie, a non-commissioned officer of the Queen's regiment, gave orders, supported by Hullin, Marceau, and others; two small pieces of cannon were brought up, the soldiers and some few citizens formed elbow to elbow, the guns were wheeled opposite the great drawbridge in the face of the musketry, and at that the Bastille gave up. De Launay made an attempt to explode his magazine, but was stopped by his men. The white flag was displayed, the drawbridge was let down, and the besiegers poured in.

Great disorder followed. De Launay and one of his officers were massacred despite the efforts of Elie and the soldiers. The uproar of Paris was intensified by the victory. At the opposite side of the city there had been another success; the Invalides had been taken and with it 30,000 muskets. With these the civic guard was rapidly being armed, under the direction of the committee of the sections. The Hotel de Ville was the centre of excitement, and the provost of the merchants, having lost all authority, was anxious to surrender his power to the new insurrectional government. Late in the evening he too was sacrificed to the violence of the mob, and, drawn from the Hotel de Ville, was quickly massacred by the worst and most excitable elements of the populace.

CHAPTER VI

FROM VERSAILLES TO PARIS

THE effect of the insurrection of Paris was immediate. Besenval, lacking instructions and intimidated by the violence of the rising, held his troops back; while Louis, shrinking from violence as he always did, and alarmed at the desertion in the army, decided to bow before the storm. He had nerved himself to a definite and resolute policy, but the instant that policy had come to the logical proof of blood-letting, he had fallen away; his kindliness, his incapacity for action, had asserted themselves strongly.

Necker was once more recalled, and once more weakly lent himself to what was rapidly becoming a farcical procedure. The King, without ceremony, presented himself to the National Assembly and announced that in view of the events of the day before he had recalled his minister, and ordered Besenval's troops to be withdrawn. The assembly manifested its satisfaction, and sent a deputation headed by

Bailly to communicate this good news to Paris. And on the same day began the first movement of emigration of the defeated courtier caste, headed by the Comte d' Artois and de Breteuil.

The deputation from the assembly presently reached Paris, and was received by the committee of the sections at the Hotel de Ville. There followed congratulation, speech-making, disorder, and excitement; and out of it the insurrection evolved a political head and a military leader, Bailly and La Fayette.

Bailly was proposed and acclaimed as Mayor of Paris. This office was new, and therefore revolutionary, but as the provost of the merchants had clearly gone for all time, it was necessary to find something to replace him, and what could be better than this? The new mayor had as qualifications for his office two facts only: he was the senior deputy of the city to the National Assembly; he possessed an unquenchable supply of civic and complimentary eloquence. Behind this figurehead the sections soon built up a new municipality or town council made up of delegates from the sections, and that varied in numbers at different times.

Paris also required a military leader, and for that post the name of the Marquis de La Fayette was acclaimed. La Fayette is a personage easy to praise or to blame, but not to estimate justly. At this moment he enjoyed all the prestige of his brilliant connection with the cause of American independence ten years before, and of his constancy to the idea of liberty. His enemies, and they were many in Court circles, could detect easily enough the vanity that entered into his composition, but neither they nor his friends could recognise or appreciate in him that truest liberalism of all which is toleration. La Fayette had already learned the lesson it took France a century to learn, that liberty implies freedom of opinion for others, and that reasonable compromise is the true basis of constructive politics. When later he appeared to swerve, or to contradict himself, it was often enough merely because he felt the scruples of a true devotee of liberty, against imposing a policy. For the moment he had become a popular idol, the generous, brave, high-minded young knight, champion of the popular cause. He was to command the civic guards of the city of Paris, 40,000 armed citizens, the national guards as they became owing to the rest of France following the example of Paris. His first act was to give them a cockade, by adding the King's white to the city's red and blue, thus forming the same tricolour that he had already fought under in another struggle for liberty ten years before.

The King's withdrawal of the troops implied a policy of conciliation, and he was therefore unable to resist the demand that he should demonstrate his acceptance of the events of Paris by a formal visit to the city. Reluctant, and half expecting violence, he made his entry on the 17th between lines of armed citizens representing every class of his Parisian subjects, and proceeded to the Hotel de Ville. It was an occasion on which a little kingly grace or a little kingly boldness, which so many of his ancestors commanded, might have fired the flame of pent-up popular emotion. But there was nothing of this sort to be found in the apathetic Louis. Bailly's stores of oratory had to be drawn on freely for what the King found himself unable to supply, and the honours of the day, which he might so easily have had, were heaped instead on the dashing La Fayette. As it was, Louis returned safely to Versailles, having met with a not unfriendly reception, but having failed to adjust himself to the new situation, which was what he was bound to attempt, having once abandoned the policy of repression by force.

The uproar of the 14th of July could not be suddenly changed to a calm, whatever Louis XVI, La Fayette and Bailly might do. Grave disorders broke out in many parts of France, and scenes of violence continued in Paris. On the 20th, Count Lally moved a resolution for the repression of the excesses that were being committed, but the assembly, with no sense of responsibility for the conduct of affairs,—directly interested, on the contrary, in weakening the executive,—defeated it. In Paris, these scenes culminated on the 23rd, when Foulon, who had been Controleur des Finances, was brought in to the city from his country estate, where he had been seized. Foulon represented all that was worst in the old régime. As commissary with the French armies and later in the internal administration of the country, he had displayed the most heartless rapacity. His attitude towards the lower classes was echoed in utterances that were popularly quoted. The people, he declared, might feed on hay while he was minister;—the people had now got him in their clutches. In vain Bailly and Lafayette, during a long agony at the Hotel de Ville, attempted to save him; the mob would not be denied. Finally Foulon was seized; he was strung up to a street lantern, and later his head, the mouth stuffed full of hay and nettles, was paraded in triumph through the streets.

While such scenes were being enacted in Paris, and while all through France the large class of poor and criminals created by Bourbonism was committing even worse excesses, the assembly was addressing itself to the task of regenerating France by endowing her with a constitution. This task appeared comparatively simple and was taken up with a light heart; it was only by degrees that the assembly discovered the difficulties in the way, and it proved to be only after two years of hard labour that it could get its constitution accomplished. And even then it proved almost useless.

The Constitution may be left for the present, to be considered when, in 1791, it became operative. The general trend of the assembly, however, was to dissociate itself from practical concerns of government, to interest itself in the theories of politics, and both in its attitude toward the events of the day, and in its constitutional policy, to weaken the executive. The executive and the Bourbon régime were synonymous, and so the men of the National Assembly, with no responsibility as it seemed for the good government of France, tried hard, at the moment when a vigorous and able executive was more than necessary, to pull down the feeble one that existed. It was the Nemesis that Bourbonism had brought on itself.

In the midst of these debates the practical question of disorder thrust itself forward once more in very insistent form, and with very remarkable results, on the night of the 4th of August. In parts of France the excitement had taken the form of a regular Jacquerie in which the isolated country houses and families of the aristocracy had suffered most. Details were accumulating and a terrible picture was unfolded before the assembly that night. How was the evil to be dealt with?

It was the injured themselves who indicated the remedy, at their own personal sacrifice. The nobles of the assembly, led by Noailles, d' Aiguillon, Beauharnais, Lameth, La Rochefoucauld, declared that if the people had attacked the property of the nobles, it was because that property represented the iniquities of feudalism, that the fault lay there, and that the remedy was not to repress the people but to suppress the institution. They therefore proposed to the Assembly that instead of issuing proclamations calling on the people to restore order, it should vote decrees for the abolition of feudalism.

And so feudalism, or what passed by the name, went by the board amid scenes of wild enthusiasm. All the seigneurial rights accumulated during a thousand years by the dominant military caste, the right of justice, the privilege of commanding armies, the hunting privileges, the warren, the dovecot, serfage,. were sacrificed on the altar of patriotic regeneration. The burden of the centuries was suddenly lifted from the shoulders of *Jacques Bonhomme*.

The men who proposed this surrender of their rights, who had already, by joining the Tiers, done so much to accomplish the great social revolution, deserve greater consideration as a class than history has, as a rule, meted out to them. The French nobility at the close of the 18th century counted in its ranks a great number of admirable men, admirable for loyalty, for intellectuality, for generosity. It is true that the most conspicuous, those who made up the Court, or who secured the lucrative appointments, had caught the plague of Versailles, and that even in the provincial nobility there was much copying of the fashion of the courtiers. But there were other representatives of the order. Most conspicuous was that large class of liberal nobles who played so great a part in the early days of the Revolution. The ten deputies elected by the nobility of Paris to the States-General all belonged to that category: grave, educated men, writers and thinkers, versed in questions of politics, economics, religion and education, experienced in many details of practical government, soldiers and local administrators, penetrated with the thought of a protesting and humanitarian age. Some, like La Fayette, had played conspicuous roles, and proved revolution in the making; others, like La Rochefoucauld, had mastered every intricacy of political and philanthropic thought; and some, like Condorcet, had proved themselves among the masters of science of their time. Counts, marquises, dukes, they were prepared to lay all aside in the overwhelming demand which suffering humanity made for release from all its troubles. And alongside of these, more loyal to their King if less loyal to humanity, no less admirable if lagging a little in knowledge and development, were those hundreds of country gentlemen, many of them poor, who, when the day of adversity came, rallied to their sovereigns, faced the guillotine for them, or laid down their lives following the fearless standard of Henri de La Rochejacquelein. The position of the French nobility, and the part it played, has been too much forgotten. Its most intelligent section nearly led the Revolution, which later fell into the hands of lawyers and theorists, then of demagogues, and lastly of soldiers.

What has just been said does not imply that the action of the National Assembly on the night of the 4th of August was altogether admirable. The example of the nobles was infectious. A consuming fervour of self-sacrifice seized every member of the house. Archbishops, bishops and abbots rushed to the tribune and offered all they could. Tithes, pluralities, and every sort of ecclesiastical privilege were sacrificed. The unprivileged class attempted desperately, but in vain, to hold its own in the contest, and could find nothing more to surrender than some of the special privileges and franchises attached to certain provinces and cities of the kingdom.

Now all this was generous and admirable,—it forms one of the most generous and admirable pages in history. It was even more. It was the emphatic and right declaration that privilege and class distinction was the root of all the evils of the old system and had been condemned by the French nation. But it had none of the qualities of practical statesmanship. It did not tend to decrease disorder but the contrary; and for the moment, with reform advancing so prosperously, order was the first consideration. The effects of the decrees were disastrous and intensified the bad conditions of the country. The woodlands were immediately invaded by armies of timber and fuel cutters. Game was killed off. The poor country priest found his salary gone. The *gabelle* itself was disregarded. Local justice came to an end. And so the Government, with all its extra load, found the already failing revenue almost entirely cut off. The peasants and people of France interpreted the decrees after their fashion, refused to pay taxes and abused the surrendered privileges.

Through August and September the assembly continued its constitutional debates, one of the three actors in this great political tragedy; the other two, Paris and King Louis, watched its proceedings with growing impatience. Uneasy at the increasing unrest of the capital, at the now popular cry that the King ought to reside in Paris, and at the constitutional demands which the assembly was gradually formulating and accumulating, Louis decided to bring some troops into Versailles for his protection, this duty being assigned to the regiment of Flanders. This was a small enough matter when compared with the formidable preparations of de Broglie and Besenval three months before, yet it served the purpose of immediately crystallizing two opposite currents of opinion.

In Paris suffering was intense. There had been a good harvest, and in many respects the economic situation was better. But there was a drought, and the millers, depending on water to drive their mills, could not produce flour. There had been a sudden curtailment of Court and aristocratic expenditure, so that the Parisian wage earner was unemployed. The emigration had thrown many retainers out of their places. Paris was starving even before the summer months were over, and the agitators and political leaders were not slow to point to Versailles as the cause. That city, owing to the King's presence, was always comparatively well supplied with provisions; if only Louis could be brought to the capital, Versailles might starve and Paris would fatten. And winter was fast coming on.

At the palace of Versailles offended pride and rebounding hope were going out to the regiment of Flanders. On the 1st of October the crisis was reached. On that day the assembly sent to the King a declaration of rights to which his assent was demanded. In the evening a banquet was given in the palace to bring together the officers of the King's bodyguard, of the regiment of Flanders and of the national guards of Versailles; and it resulted in a demonstration. The King and Queen visited the assembled officers and were received with great enthusiasm. *O Richard, o mon Roi,* the air that Blondel sings to Richard, the imprisoned king of England, in the then popular opera by Grétry, was sung, and officers of the national guard were moved to change their tricolour cockade for the white one of the King. All this, if not very dangerous, was exciting; it was immensely magnified by rumour. In Paris the popular orators soon conjured up visions of a great royalist plot, and the renewal of military operations against the city.

On the 5th of October, the King, struggling against the pressure of the assembly, sent in a conditional acceptance of the proposals of the 1st, making some reservations as to the declaration of rights. He did not know that at the very moment Paris had risen once more, and was already marching out to Versailles to carry him off and bring him back to the capital.

The insurrection of the 5th of October had rather obscure origins. Some of its leading factors, however, stand out clearly enough. First there was the slowly rising tide of the popular impatience, the feeling that after all the efforts and success of the spring and summer the situation of affairs was still no better, and that to improve it the King must come to Paris; all this increasing vastly in force since the 1st of October. Then there was the fact that Paris knew on the evening of the 4th, that Louis would refuse, or in part refuse, the demands of the assembly, and it was necessary, therefore, to find a reply to the King's move. Last of all was hunger. And it was the part of the Parisian people most nearly touched by hunger that actually raised the standard of revolt.

The women felt the pinch of famine more bitterly than the men, and the women played a noteworthy part in the formation of those deep strata of popular opinion, or instinct, on which in turn each of the revolutionary parties had to build their power. The women were the first to turn the cannon against the King, and they were the last to raise the horrible howl of the guillotine at the prisoners as they passed the prison gates to go to the scaffold. And the reason is not far to seek. It was they who had to look after the household, to tend the sick, to feed the children, and it was they who day after day, year after year, formed in the long procession waiting to reach the baker's or the butcher's stall. Often enough they stood and struggled for hours, sometimes through the whole night, their hearts aching for the loved ones at home,—at the end of all to find nothing left, to return empty-handed. So late as the year 1795 there was a period of several months during which the individual ration, for those who could pay and for those who were lucky, was but 2 oz. of black bread a day; while butcher's meat failed completely on many occasions and was always a costly luxury. The details of the famine are scattered broadly through the pages of the contemporaries, and at every point the woman appears, wretched, lamenting, furious, ravenous for food, fighting for it and plundering, her heart dulled with bitterness, and her mouth distorted with curses for those pointed out to her as the cause of all her sufferings. Louis, Marie Antoinette, Brissot, Vergniaud, Hébert, she cared little what the name was, but was equally ready to rend them when told that they stood for the starvation of her children, her sick, or her husband. And she was easily enough persuaded that some one person was responsible. In the morning hours of the 6th of October she was convinced that Louis was that person.

In the early hours of that day a knot of women, one of them beating a drum, others lugubriously chanting *du pain, du pain,* bread, bread, appeared in the streets of Paris. Growing in numbers as they advanced, an inchoate mob of women, men and boys, they proceeded to the Hotel de Ville; there perhaps they would find relief? But there was no relief, only tumult, until Maillard, a patriot agitator, conspicuous as one of the captors of the Bastille and since, harangued them. Maillard, who was in touch with the leading spirits among the politicians of the sections, told the women that there was nothing to do at the Hotel de Ville, but that he would lead them to Versailles, where they could see the King and persuade him to give them bread and to come back with them to Paris.

A motley procession poured out from Paris, following Maillard into the country roads and villages on the way to Versailles. Armed men had joined the women, and a few cannon had been found and were dragged by hand.

Meanwhile La Fayette, always sent for in emergencies, had arrived at the Hotel de Ville; while alarming reports began to reach Versailles of the approach of the women of Paris. La Fayette was quickly joined by a large force of national guards, and while he awaited instructions and pacified them with occasional harangues, Bailly and his councillors debated as to what course to take. Finally about five in the afternoon it was decided that La Fayette and his men should proceed to Versailles to preserve order and act according to circumstances.

Long before the Parisian troops could arrive, Versailles had been taken by storm by the women. They tramped in under a beating rain, many having lagged or fallen exhausted by the way, and at once sent deputations to the assembly and the King. They wanted food, and they wanted decrees that would put an end to starvation. To the men of the regiment of Flanders, drawn up to protect the palace, they announced the same thing, and their appeals were so irresistible that after some hours the colonel of the regiment, on declaring that he could not answer for his men any longer, got permission to return to barracks.

But by this time La Fayette had reached the scene, and had stationed his battalions so as to protect the palace. An anxious night was passed. In the mob were very dangerous elements. The grilles and walls, the courts, the grounds and the buildings of the palace, covered a wide area. The organization for defence was defective; the *gardes du corps* were trustworthy but not numerous; the King gave few orders, and those benevolent or timid; the unrest and pressure of the mob was irresistible. In the early hours of the morning a determined group of men got into the palace, and immediately began to force their way towards the Queen's apartment.

As the 6th of October opened, a scene of great excitement took place within the palace. *Gardes du corps* were cut down while protecting the Queen's flight to the King's apartments. La Fayette was sent for in haste, and some sort of order was restored. But meanwhile the mob had invaded the main courtyard, and it required all La Fayette's great popularity and tact to avert a fatal outbreak. As it was, he persuaded Louis that the only course was to accept the popular demand for his removal to Paris; he harangued the mob; he induced the

King and Queen to show themselves at a window; he gracefully kissed the Queen's hand; and he eventually prevailed.

At noon Paris began to flow back from Versailles to the capital once more, but now Louis and his family were in the midst of the throng. In a great lumbering coach, surrounded by the populace, Louis and his wife and children were proceeding from the palace of Versailles to that of the Tuileries; an epoch of French history was coming to a close. The Austrian princess, looking out and seeing a man of the people riding on the step of her coach, declared contemptuously that this was the first occasion on which an individual not wearing knee breeches, an individual *sans culotte,* had occupied so honourable a position. The cry of *sans culotte* was taken up, and approved on the spot as the symbol of worthy citizenship. But the cant phrase that belongs most closely to the event of the 6th of October, was that whereby the Parisians declared triumphantly that they had now brought into their midst *le boulanger, la boulangère, et le petit mitron,*—the baker, the baker's wife and the little cook boy.

CHAPTER VII

THE ASSEMBLY DEMOLISHES PRIVILEGE

IN the preceding chapter, stress has been laid on the economic causes that had led to the rooting up of the Bourbons from Versailles; in this one the political significance of the event must be accentuated. In the history of the Revolution it is always so; the political and the economic factors are constantly fusing the one in the other.

In a sense, what had happened was that the poor people, the democracy, let us say, of Paris, had now got the King in the city and under their influence; not only the King, but also the assembly,—for it had followed Louis and was installed in a building adjacent to the Tuileries. And the assembly became quickly conscious of the fact that Paris was now unduly weighing on the representation of France, and under the lead of Mirabeau attempted to assert itself. This was the first feeble step towards the assumption of power that culminated three years later in the appointment of the Committee of Public Safety. The assembly assumed a middle position between the King on the one hand and the mob on the other. It voted the change of Louis' title from King of France, by the grace of God, to King of the French, by virtue of the Constitution; it repressed disorder by proclaiming martial law; but in the continuation of its constitutional debates it asserted unequivocally its middle-class composition. A handful of democrats, Robespierre, Grégoire, and less than a dozen others, pleaded the rights of the many, but the assembly declined to listen to them and confirmed, by a nearly unanimous vote, the recommendations of its committees for drawing up the declaration of rights and constitution. The greater part of French citizens were thereby declared to have only passive, not active rights, and were excluded from the franchise. The qualification for voting was placed at the paying of taxes equal to 3 days' labour, and for being a deputy paying in taxes one marc of silver, about 54 francs.

The outcry against this legislation was so loud, and so widespread, as to show what genuine political aspirations were to be found in the mass of the Parisian population. The greater part of that population was excluded from voting. For to say nothing of the fact that about 120,000 inhabitants were classed as paupers, it so happened that the capitation tax had been remitted for a term of years, leaving only the well-to-do shopkeeper, some part of the professional, and the capitalist class on the voters' list. Workmen of the faubourg St. Antoine signed a petition to be allowed to pay taxes so as to obtain a vote. Robespierre, a narrow, prudish, jealous, puritanical but able lawyer from Arras, with journalists like Desmoulins and Loustallot, inveighed against what they described as iniquitous class legislation that would have excluded from the councils of the French nation Jean Jacques Rousseau and even that *pauvre sans culotte* Jesus Christ. But the assembly was obdurate, and, in fact, remained middle class in its point of view all through the Revolution except when irresistible pressure was brought to bear against it.

The journalists, however, tended far more rapidly towards democracy than the deputies. Journalism had sprung from the events of July. The pamphlets of Camille Desmoulins had, by a natural metamorphosis, become journals after that date. Their popularity did not, however, attain that of Loustallot's *Révo-*

lutions de Paris, of which one number is said to have reached a circulation of 200,000. Marat's *Ami du peuple,* first published in September, soon became the most formidable organ of opinion, and remained so until the rise of Hébert and his atrocious *Père Duchesne,* at a later period. These papers and their editors played a great part, and will often be noticed, but for the present all that need be said is that their rise at this period is one of the symptoms of the tremendous change that had come over the city of Paris.

Paris before 1789 was, in a sense, mediæval, provincial. Although the largest city of France, its capital, the centre of thought and art, the resort of many French and foreign visitors, the city was still in a way a local centre, and isolated, unrelated with the rest of France. The Court did not reside there, the administration, especially of justice, was in large measure decentralized, and Paris was the abode of the Parisian almost in the same narrow sense that the province was the abode of the provincial. But now all this was rapidly changing. The arrival of the Court and of the National Assembly suddenly made of Paris the heart of France. The fever of revolution made that heart beat faster, and a rapid current of the best life blood of the nation began circulating from the provinces to Paris and from Paris back again to the provinces, bringing energy and a broadening of sympathy with it. And if a glance is taken at Europe during the same period, during the twenty-five years that follow the outbreak of the French Revolution, the same process may be seen at work, but on a larger scale. The old stagnation, the feudal congestion of Germany and Italy, the immobility of the population, is broken through, the old barriers are shaken down; great centralized states send official, economic, and national action sweeping back and forth; great armies tramp through the whole breadth of Europe; roads are built in all directions to facilitate their movements, people begin to know one another, to mix, to form larger conceptions of humanity.

The most potent of the agencies that effected this change in Paris was the direct work of the deputies themselves. The move to the capital had been attended by the formation of several well-marked currents of opinion among the deputies. One of these had been a movement of protest,—of protest and in part of timidity. The violence and compulsion applied to the King, and all that the removal to Paris implied under such circumstances, had led to the withdrawal of about 200 members of the assembly. Of these Mounier was the chief; he returned to his province of Dauphiné and attempted to provoke constitutional action to free the King from the domination of Paris. His efforts were unsuccessful and he eventually had to leave the country. This group, however, of which Mounier was the boldest member, represented merely a negative force, dispersion; another, equally large, stood for something more concrete.

The Club Breton began to develop very rapidly after the removal to Paris. Its members, styling themselves *Amis de la Constitution,* eventually settled themselves in quarters conveniently near the palace at the Jacobin monastery. Here the club quickly became a debating association, and the headquarters of a party. Early in 1790 it began to develop a system of affiliating clubs all through France, and by August of that year had planted 150 Jacobin colonies in direct correspondence with the mother society. By 1794 this number had grown to a thousand, and Jacobinism had become a creed. But in 1789 and 1790 the Jacobins were as yet moderate in their views; they were the men who wanted to create a constitution under the monarchy; they were presided during that period by such men as the Duc de Noailles, the Duc d' Aiguillon and Mirabeau.

Mirabeau stood out in the assembly as the one constructive statesman, the one man who might bridge the gulf that still separated the deputies from the responsibility of power and the practice of government. If a constitutional or parliamentary ministry were possible, if both King and assembly would recognise in that the practical step towards re-establishing order and making reform effective, Mirabeau was the necessary leader of such a ministry. In the period that followed the arrival of the King in Paris he amply demonstrated both his qualifications and his defects for such a position. Urgent questions pressed the assembly from all sides, and in debating them Mirabeau took a lion's share.

Finance was most urgent of all. Necker could do no more. A fundamental remedy for the needs of the exchequer must be found. On the 7th of October the assembly had voted that the Crown lands should become the property of the nation, in return for which a civil list would be assigned to the King. Three days later Talleyrand-Périgord, the sceptical but able Bishop of Autun, proposed that the property of the Church should be similarly dealt with. This was, in one sense, as the previous step had been, the assertion of the national interest over the special privilege; in another sense it was merely one step more in those numerous secularizations of Church property which the utilitarian and unreligious 18th century had carried out. It was proposed to take over for the use of the State all the property of the Church and in return to pay salaries to its priests. This represented the acquisition of real property valued at the capital sum of 2,100,000,000 of francs; but as it only brought in capital value, not cash in hand, it did not afford any immediate relief for the needs of the Government. Then another expedient was tried, the appeal for patriotic gifts, and that, though it resulted in a good deal of patriotic emotionalism, did little to fill the yawning gulf of bankruptcy. Finally in December, drastic measures were taken. Some of the State's payments were provisionally suspended; the sale of Church and other lands to the value of 400 millions was ordered; a loan of 80 millions was sanctioned; and 400 millions of *assignats* were issued.

The assignat in this first form was an inchoate mortgage bond. It bore interest; it was guaranteed by the State; it purported to be secured in a general way on the national property; and it was to circulate as money and to be accepted in payment for the national lands. If it had been strictly secured, on a close valuation, and by a registered claim against specified property, it would doubtless have given a permanent support to the finances of the Government. As it was it proved, at first, a successful step, and it was only by gradual stages and from unwise measures that it eventually failed. In April 1790, assignats were made legal tender; a few months later they ceased to bear interest,—in other words, though still bonds on their face they really became paper money. In September 1790, another 800 millions were issued, and in June another 600, and in small denominations, and from that moment they began to sink in value rapidly. Until the month of January 1791 they stood at over 90; in July 1791 they were at 87; during 1792–93, years of the greatest crisis, they fell fast; in 1795 they had almost lost value and during the Directoire period the assignat becomes almost worthless, one recorded transaction giving 3,080 francs in paper for 20 in gold.

Behind the financial policy of the assembly was Mirabeau. He had long been connected with the bankers and promoters of Paris, had produced pamphlets to serve their financial projects. The bond issues of the assembly, and the probable sales of large blocks of real property, were of great interest to these groups, and Mirabeau was their natural connecting link with the assembly. He was the strongest advocate of the assignat measures, and whatever interest his friends took in them, it need not be doubted that he believed them salutary and wise.

The Court in its new perplexity, helplessly entangled in Paris, having learnt just a little from experience, now turned to Mirabeau for assistance. He secretly advised that the King should take the initiative, and should put forward the policy of a moderate constitution on the English model with a responsible ministry. If this brought on a conflict, or if his situation otherwise made it advisable to leave Paris, he should seek refuge in the well-disposed province of Normandy, and not with the army on the German frontier. The advice of Mirabeau was not unsound, and it implied as a step the formation of a Mirabeau, Necker, La Fayette ministry.

But Mirabeau was too much handicapped by his past. The Assembly viewed him with rooted suspicion and dislike, and for this reason the Court could not have chosen a worse agent. At the end of November the assembly voted decrees excluding its members from the King's ministry, thus barring Mirabeau's path, and thus accentuating once more its own destructive attitude towards the Government. If it would not participate, even indirectly, in the executive, it was partly because it was at heart anxious to pull that executive down to earth.

Notwithstanding this check, Mirabeau continued to impose on the assembly by his tremendous personality and by his statesmanship. He struggled hard in the early part of 1790 to bring the deputies into line on a question of foreign affairs that then arose,— the Nootka Sound question. This involved all the traditions of France's foreign policy and her system of alliances, the *pacte de famille;* but the assembly saw in it merely a text on which to formulate the limitations it intended to impose on the royal power in the matter of foreign relations. At this moment the Court had renewed its clandestine communications with Mirabeau, there was even one secret interview between him and the Queen, and large sums were given him as payment for his advice. These sums he squandered profusely, thus advertising a fact that was already more than suspected by the public, and rapidly destroying his hold on opinion.

The winter was a much milder one than the preceding, food was less scarce, money more plentiful owing to the issue of assignats, public confidence greatly increased. But the tension between the King and the assembly did not relax; there was no serious attempt on either side to take advantage of the improved situation for effecting a reconciliation. The assembly legislated against the members of the aristocracy who, following the example of the Comte d' Artois, had emigrated. Instead of helping the Government to enforce police measures that would have made their residence in France secure, it decreed the confiscation of their rents unless they returned within three months. This was the first of a long series of laws aimed against the *émigrés*.

Turning from one privileged order to the other, the assembly continued the attacks on the fabric of the Church which had been begun by the churchmen themselves in August and October 1789. The surrender of the tithes,

70,000,000 francs annually, had told most heavily against the poor country priest and in favour of the landowner, who bore the burden of his salary. The taking over of the Church lands by the State had been most felt by the higher ecclesiastics and the monastic orders. In February 1790 the latter were suppressed, and their members were relieved of their vows by the assembly, which had now frankly embarked on an anti-clerical policy. It would not recognise of itself that it was less representative of France in the matter of religion than in any other; for it was the intellectual and professional class only, to which nearly all the deputies belonged, that was Voltairian or anti-Catholic, the mass of the people of France were still attached to their ancient faith. During the protracted debates that took place on the Church question in the spring of 1790, the assembly attempted several times to evade the question of the Catholic members as to whether or not it would recognise the existence of the Church. At last, with great reluctance, in June, the assembly voted that the Catholic religion was that of France; but it followed this up by passing what was known as the *Constitution civile du clergé.* This decree provided that all priests should receive their salaries from the State; that the old dioceses of France should be broken up and made to fit the new departmental division that had supplanted the old provincial one; that the bishop should be created by the vote of the electors of his department; and that the Pope should exercise no authority over bishops or priests.

It needs but little acquaintance with history to realize how wilfully subversive this plan was. The maintenance of the clergy by the tithes, placed it outside the sphere of Government control, and helped to maintain the ancient Roman internationalism; whereas the breaking off of the Pope's direct connection with the bishops was Gallicanism of the most pronounced character. Pope Pius VI unequivocally declared that the carrying through of any such law in France would amount to a schism, and transmitted that opinion to Louis XVI.

The falseness of the King's position was made intolerable by the dilemma in which he was now placed. There was as yet no formal Constitution, only a revolutionary situation in which the assembly had usurped a large part of the King's prerogative. It was, however, virtually accepted by both sides that under the constitution when passed, the King should have the power of veto, and by tacit accord that arrangement had been from the first put into force. The assembly voted decrees and sent them to the King for his signature. But in reality the veto, even before its strict constitutional existence, was little more than a sham. The situation was revolutionary. Both parties were hostile, and almost without exception every signature of the King was an act of moral compulsion. Hitherto, however, his acceptance of the situation had not involved more than bowing before a political storm; now the matter was graver, the question was of schism, and therefore of heresy.

Louis was a faithful believer in the Roman theology, as well as in the divine right of kings, and he struggled hard to withhold his signature from the civil constitution of the clergy. And when, after some weeks, he finally gave in, it was under protest. From that moment he adopted the attitude of the man acting under restraint who ascribes no binding force to acts and deeds resulting from compulsion.

The acceptance of the civil constitution of the clergy by the King did not conclude the matter. Furious protests arose. In the south of France, bishops, priests and national guards for some weeks threatened an outbreak of religious war. The assembly met this disorder more firmly than that proceeding from economic and political reasons. Towards the close of the year it imposed on the clergy an oath of adhesion to the civil constitution, and this only four bishops were found to accept. In January 1791 elections were ordered for filling the places of those members of the Church who had refused the oath, and presently France found herself with two bodies of clergy, official and non-official, constitutional and anti-constitutional.

To close a chapter dealing so largely with the destructive efforts of the middle-class assembly against the prerogatives of the King and of the two privileged orders, it may be noted that on the 19th of June, 1790, on the proposal of members of the nobility, all titles were abolished. Hereafter Mirabeau is Honoré Riquetti, the *ci-devant* Comte de Mirabeau; and Camille Desmoulins, prompt, picturesque and impertinent, logically applies the process to the King himself and rechristens Louis, *Mr. Capet l'ainé*.

CHAPTER VIII

THE FLIGHT TO VARENNES

ON the 14th of July 1790 was held the first great festival of the Revolution, the federation of the national guards at the Champ de Mars in Paris. Federation was the name that had been given all through France the previous year to district or departmental gatherings or reviews, at which the newly raised national guards had paraded and, with great ceremony, sworn patriotic oaths. This was now repeated on a grander and more centralized scale, to commemorate the fall of the Bastille twelve months before. On the military exercise ground just outside Paris, 14,000 national guards assembled. An altar was erected, at which Talleyrand, Bishop of Autun and deputy, officiated. La Fayette led the military procession. Louis was made to play an almost subordinate role. The national guards took an oath of fidelity to La Fayette, the Law, and Louis XVI; the gradation was intended and significant.

The festival was, in a sense, merely an echo of the policy which the assembly was pursuing in regard to the army. The army was a great factor in the situation; sooner or later, as in most revolutions, it was likely to prove the decisive one. From the first the pressure of the armed force on Paris had acted as a powerful irritant; and in reducing the power of the King nothing seemed more important than to detach the army from its allegiance. The mutiny and desertion of July 1789 gave the assembly a good starting point; in the spring of 1790 the troops were placed under oath to obey the law and the King, and not to act against the citizens. This, however, was not decisive, for on the northeastern frontier, far from Paris, among the fortresses of Alsace and Lorraine, a considerable part of the army was assembled. There French and foreign regiments were well mixed, esprit de corps was maintained, staunch loyalists were in command, and it was conceivable that the troops would respond to Louis' appeal if the King summoned them to his help.

So thought Marat, and many others. The author of the *Ami du peuple* voiced the popular fear, that the army on the northeastern frontier would destroy the national cause. Everything in Marat's career tended to make him the accredited prophet of the reign of suspicion now fast becoming established. He had during many years studied science and philosophy, and had acquired the knack of writing while unsuccessfully knocking at the doors of the academies. The outbreak of the Revolution found him soured, and ready to turn a venomous pen against all detainers of power. A morbid streak fast developed into a mania of persecution and suspicion, and it was by giving free rein to his imagination in that respect that he came into line with the frenzy of starving women and declaiming demagogues ready to believe every accusation, and to rend every *accapareur*.

Marat's violence had become so great shortly after the taking of the Bastille that he had been proceeded against by the new municipality of Paris. He then began a life of hiding, flitting obscurely from point to point, dwelling in cellars, even at one time concealing himself in a drain. For a few weeks he fled to London. But in the spring of 1790 he was back in Paris, and at the crisis of the midsummer he published a violent pamphlet, *C'en est fait de nous,* "it's all up with us," in which he hysterically demanded the massacre of all traitors and conspirators as the only means of preserving Paris from the vengeance of the King and the operations of his army.

The assembly denounced the pamphlet, and steps were taken for the prosecution of its author. Marat had chosen the moment for his denunciations badly, for within a few days of the publication of his pamphlet the army had broken out in open mutiny against its generals. Bouillé, a staunch royalist and experienced soldier, was in command. His men were being gradually demoralized by democratic propaganda. At last, on the 31st of August, several regiments in garrison at Nancy broke out in mutiny.

Bouillé displayed great vigour in dealing with a difficult and dangerous crisis. He forced his way into Nancy after severe fighting, and dealt summarily with the offenders when once he had regained control. One French regiment he disbanded. The Swiss regiment of Chateauvieux he handed over to a court-martial of its officers, who ordered a great number of their men to be shot, or to be sent to the galleys.

These events caused great excitement. The assembly, now alarmed at the result of its own work of disintegration, passed a formal vote of thanks to Bouillé. The democratic party, however, took the opposite side, strongly led by the Cordeliers, a popular sectional club. Noisy demonstrations followed in favour of the defeated soldiers, and license and indiscipline were extolled as the virtues of free men. This more than anything else broke down the old royal army, and from this moment the cavalry and infantry officers began to throw up their commissions and emigrate. And, incidentally, another fragment of the old régime disappeared in the same storm; Necker, still a royal minister, unimportant and discredited, was mobbed on the 2d of September, and as a result resigned and ingloriously left France for his native Switzerland.

Until the winter of 1790 the Revolution had not shown signs of becoming anti-monarchical, but at the turn of the year republicanism at last raised its head. In the attitude of the French towards this question one must bear in mind the historical precedents before them. French opinion was strongly impregnated with the apparent lessons of the great revolution that had occurred in England a little more than one hundred years before. There a republic, founded in revolt from incompetent monarchy, had failed, and had made way for a military dictatorship, which also had failed, to be replaced by the restored monarchy. And, last of all, eventual success had come from a bargain or compromise between the upper and middle class on the one hand and the King on the other. This was the historic precedent best known and generally uppermost in the minds of the men of the national assembly.

But there was another precedent, that of the American revolution, and it tended in the opposite direction. Few, indeed, perceived that Washington had succeeded where Cromwell had failed; and the event was too near in time, too distant in space, too remote in surroundings, to have as much bearing as it should. Yet the impression made was considerable. Benjamin Franklin's picturesque and worthy republicanism was not forgotten: his plain clothes and robust sense, his cheerful refrain of *ça ira,*—it's all right,—so soon to be the song of the French republicans themselves. The men of Rochambeau's army too, had caught the infection, had seen republicanism in war, the brave and capable commanding whatever their station in life; and in that army were many rankers, held down by the Bourbon régime, who were soon to become the victorious generals of the French Republic. Again the constitutional documents of the Americans had been consulted, studied,—declarations of right, State constitutions. And all this tended towards republicanism.

Yet even the American example did not mean republicanism in the democratic sense. And the movement that became so marked about December 1790 was distinctly towards a democratic republic. Many prominent journalists were of that way of thought. Desmoulins had been even in 1789. The franchise restrictions which the assembly was drafting into the Constitution gave the papers a good text. It was pointed out that whereas all Frenchmen had been admitted to vote for the States-General, under the proposed constitution there would be but two million voters. Why should not the poor man have a vote? Why should not even women have a vote? Should there not be equality of rights and no invidious distinctions?

Pamphlets began to appear in favour of a republic. Popular societies were formed, and became the vogue, with a programme of universal suffrage, and fraternization as a social characteristic. Women, occasionally children, were admitted; the members called one another brother and sister, having discarded more formal modes of address; popular banquets were held. The influence of woman, of which something has already been said, was widened by the action of these societies; that influence a little later tended to give the Revolution the hysterical turn which it took.

The professional politicians showed little inclination to follow the lead of the *Sociétés populaires*. The assembly remained rigidly middle class in its attitude. The Jacobin Club maintained the same position, though a few of its members were now inclining towards democracy, and one of them, Robespierre, not quite so isolated as a few months earlier, came forward as its official mouthpiece. In April 1791 he issued a speech, printed in pamphlet form, in which he ably argued the case for democratic suffrage. He was hailed as the champion and friend of the poor man, the apostle of fraternity.

Since he had been compelled to accept the civil constitution of the clergy the King's revolt had become more marked. He declared to his friends that he would sooner be king of Metz than king of France under such terms. The rise of the democratic movement in the winter had not tended to allay his fears, and by the spring of 1791 he was decided, so far as it was in his nature ever to be decided, to remove from Paris and find some way out of his difficulties. His hopes of escape centred on the northeastern frontier. There, at Metz, 200 miles from Paris, were the headquarters of the energetic Bouillé; and beyond Metz was the Rhine, where the Emperor Leopold, his brother-in-law, was already assembling troops that might prove a further support.

With such an outlook, it was natural that the Court, and in this case the Court meant the Queen, should attempt to concert measures with Vienna; the phantom of the Austrian alliance, so detested at the time of the Seven Years' War, was reappearing. Marie Antoinette held numerous conferences with the foreign ambassadors on the subject and wrote frequent letters to her brother invoking his aid; all of which was more or less suspected or known by the public outside the palace walls.

Paris was, indeed, guarding her king very jealously. Marat constantly preached suspicion. Zealous sections formed watch committees that kept the palace under keen observation. If the King attempted to leave Paris violence must be used to keep him there. Royalists offered their protection to the King;

and in February a bad brawl took place within the palace walls, between the two factions.

Incidents kept occurring. In March the assembly voted that the King was the first public functionary, and therefore, like other functionaries, responsible for carrying out certain duties. One of these was declared to be that he must reside within 20 leagues of the assembly. This measure was in one sense restrictive; in another it seemed slightly to loosen the King's fetters. To test whether he could not take advantage of this decree to enlarge his radius of movement, it was decided that Louis should attempt an afternoon's excursion as far as St. Cloud.

In all this matter Mirabeau had been consulted. His advice had been constant and correct. If the King would make his departure from Paris coincide with taking the lead in a real reform he might get most support and rouse least opposition by going to Rouen, the capital of Normandy, a very accessible point; to go to Metz was to touch the self-same chord that had whipped Paris into open revolt in July 1789.

But although Mirabeau's advice was asked, what he said was only half listened to. No one could trust him now, no one could believe him—and besides, he was dying. Battling in the assembly for measures of constructive statesmanship, spending his life outside with profuse extravagance, his vitality was now gone, and a fever carried him off on the 2d of April. His death caused a great sensation, though few would say a word of praise for the great orator. He realized that his death removed the last possible hope for the monarchy, and Louis himself, when Marie Antoinette showed her satisfaction at the news, rebuked her and declared that he had lost a friend.

Friendless, what could Louis do now? The obscure Robespierre, tortuous, fanatical and tenacious, had risen to importance; hitherto the giant Mirabeau had held down the smaller man and his little group by his breadth, his vigour and his crushing apostrophes:—*Silence aux trente voix!* But now that Mirabeau was gone, Robespierre suddenly appeared almost the first figure of the assembly; and Robespierre stood for the rising tide of democracy. What could Louis do? To escape from Paris seemed the only course.

The King had occasionally been to St. Cloud in the year 1790, and the recent edict of the assembly formally assured his freedom of movement for a much greater distance; it only remained to test whether the people of Paris would attempt to restrain him from acting in a manner that was customary and within his constitutional rights.

The test proved conclusive. A large mob, including a number of national guards, assembled at the palace on Easter Sunday. It had been announced that on this day the King would visit St. Cloud to hear mass performed by priests who had not accepted the civil constitution. He was not allowed to proceed. After sitting in his carriage several hours awaiting the moment when the mob would give him passage, he returned to his apartments defeated.

Louis was a prisoner. Not only was he a prisoner, but he was compelled by the assembly to have within the palace only priests whom he considered schismatic, and compelled to appear in the assembly and there declare solemnly that he was a free agent and enjoyed entire liberty of action. This drove him to a definite purpose, and preparations were now secretly begun for the flight to Metz.

On the 20th of June the attempt was made. The King's brother, the Comte de Provence, who afterwards became Louis XVIII, managed his escape well, and was driven over the frontier into the Netherlands,—an experience he was to repeat in 1815. The King's arrangements had been placed in the hands of a Swedish nobleman attached to the Queen, Count Fersen. False passports were obtained. The royal family was smuggled out of the palace in disguise. Several bodyguards dressed as couriers acted as escort. A large travelling carriage was ready. A start was successfully made on the great northeastern road.

All went prosperously until the fugitives reached Varennes, a village in the frontier district not more than 15 miles from Verdun, where Bouillé had a strong garrison. At this point the scheme broke down. Bouillé should have been able to place a large cavalry escort about the King's carriage at Varennes, but his arrangements were defective and went wrong. This was not altogether his fault, for Louis had wasted much precious time on the way, and had shown no sense of the resolution required by the circumstances. And lastly the patriots had discovered who the traveller was; the postmaster of Ste Ménehould had recognised the King, had ridden on ahead, had roused the national guard of Varennes—and now the game was up.

After a slight skirmish between a detachment of Bouillé's cavalry and the national guard of Varennes, Louis was started back for Paris, surrounded by armed contingents from all the near-by villages. The whole course of the Revolution had for an instant wavered, hesitating whether to turn this way or that. Now it had turned in a direction that could not be mistaken. Louis himself speaking to one of the officials of Varennes said to him: "If we return to Paris, we shall die."

It was early on the morning of the 21st of June that Paris learnt that the King had left the capital; intense excitement resulted. No doubt could be felt as to the significance of the event; the King himself had taken care that there should be none by leaving behind a lengthy proclamation of which the upshot was that all the decrees he had signed were null and void because of compulsion. The people answered this in the way that might be expected; every emblem of royalty was torn down through the city.

The assembly was in a state of the greatest uncertainty. It had two dangers to face, one from the King, immediate, another from the people, less immediate yet calling for much prudence. In this moment of crisis and doubt, numerous solutions of the political problem were put forward, of which several demand notice.

Marat, in *l' Ami du peuple,* declared that a military dictator was the only remedy for the situation; a curiously logical perception of what was to be the outcome of the Revolution. This opinion did not obtain any success.

The duc d'Orléans proposed another solution. This personage was the head of the branch of the French Bourbons that stood next to that holding the throne. He had long been on bad terms with the Court and had assiduously cultivated popularity among the Parisians. During the winter of 1788–89 he had spent much money and effort in charity and the relief of distress, and had his reward on the assembly of the States-General at which, while the Queen was received in stony silence, he had met with an ovation. He did his best to create an Orléans party, to push for the throne, and devoted to the purpose the large sums of money which his great fortune placed at his disposal. At every crisis in the Revolution small groups, mostly subsidized, attempted to provoke demonstrations in his favour. And now, on the 21st of June, with the throne derelict, he thought his opportunity had come, and ostentatiously paraded through the central quarters of the city in hopes of a popular movement. But the popular movement would not come. The duke was too well understood; his vices were too well known; his treachery to his cousin aroused no enthusiasm; the people wanted a more complete solution.

That more complete solution was voiced by the Club of the Cordeliers and by its formidable spokesman Danton. Like Mirabeau, Danton was of large physique and stentorian voice, an orator by nature, a man whose unusual if far from handsome features fascinated the crowd. But, unlike his great predecessor, he could hold the affection of the people, indeed, he proved one of the few conspicuous leaders against whom the people did not turn on the day of going to the guillotine. A lawyer, and of a lawyer's family, he was in lucrative practice when the Revolution broke out, a fine advocate, not overscrupulous in method, flexible, but large in view, generous in heart, irresistible in courage, strong in political instincts, a man of the greatest possibilities. He espoused the popular cause, and the popular cause in the democratic sense. He stood for the sections against the central Commune; he defended Marat and the liberty of the press; he opposed the bourgeois régime and La Fayette at every step; he led the battalion of the Cordeliers section to the Tuileries to prevent Louis' visit to St. Cloud in April 1791. Such was the man who now headed a deputation of the Cordeliers Club to the assembly and presented a petition demanding the deposition of Louis XVI.

The demand of the Cordeliers for the deposition of the King was not the thing to please the assembly. The situation was doubly difficult, for apart from the uncertainty as to the whereabouts of the King and the possibility of civil war, there was a difficulty in regard to the Constitution. For two years past the assembly had been labouring hard to complete the work it had sworn to accomplish by the oath of the *Jeu de Paume*. That work was now nearly completed, but was almost as unpopular with the masses as it was hateful to the King. It had not even been elaborated in a spirit of compromise between the extreme claims of autocracy on the one hand and of democracy on the other, but was frankly middle-class legislation. But the King was an essential part of the constitutional mechanism and his flight had occurred just in time to wreck the Constitution as it was coming into port—that was the prevailing sentiment of the members of the assembly. When on the 24th it was known that Louis had been stopped and was returning to Paris, the relief of the deputies was great,—their long-laboured Constitution was safe after all.

It was not till the next day that the royal family reached the capital; and before their arrival more than one exciting scene occurred. The duc d'Orléans was admitted a member of the Jacobin Club. Danton, apparently not unfriendly for the moment to d'Orléans, harangued the Jacobins in favour of the appointment of a regency. But the assembly maintained a negative attitude. It seized control of the administration by ordering the ministers, now little more than chief clerks of departments, to report to it for orders, and for the rest awaited the return of the King.

On the 25th Louis and his family reached Paris. The whole population turned out to watch his return, but it gave him no greeting. The crowd, obeying a common instinct, received the King in dead silence. Not a voice was heard, not a hat was raised, as Louis once more passed into his palace of the Tuileries.

CHAPTER IX

WAR BREAKS OUT

FROM the 25th of June to the 17th of July the conflict between the middle class and the democratic party continued with great intensity. Louis was, in reality, less the object than the pretext of their quarrel. The Cordeliers urged that France, and not the assembly, should pronounce the King's fate, and to effect that it would be necessary to proceed to a referendum, to demand a popular vote. But this was precisely what the Constitution refused to permit, and hence the demand was in reality an attack on the Constitution. Day after day the agitation grew, changing slightly in form. Finally the democrats decided on a monster petition to be signed at the altar of the Champ de Mars on the 17th of July.

Danton himself stood at one of the corners of the platform that day to help on the signing of the protest of the Parisian democracy. But Bailly, La Fayette, and the mass of the assembly had decided on a policy of repression.

The national guards arrived in strong force. Confusion followed. Volleys were fired. The mob, after losing many dead, fled for safety. Danton, escaping, left Paris and proceeded to London, where he remained until the storm had blown over. By this stroke the assembly for the moment retained control. But the situation was profoundly changed. If Danton and the popular insurrectional force were for the moment defeated, Robespierre and intellectual democracy were making rapid headway; the centre of gravity of revolutionary opinion was shifting in his direction. Just before the crisis the Jacobins had been invaded by a Palais Royal mob who had hooted down the constitutionalist speakers, and imposed their opinion on the club. This led to disruption. The moderate Jacobins left, and, at the neighbouring *Feuillants,* founded a new society that was gradually to become more and more retrograde. The few advanced Jacobins retained possession of the old club, with its great affiliation of country clubs, infused a radical element into its membership, and soon, making of Robespierre its mouthpiece and its prophet, advanced in the direction of imposing his doctrine of political salvation on France.

Meanwhile the assembly, with its constitutional keystone securely locked up in the Tuileries, was hastening to profit by its victory. The opportunity for completing the Constitution might never recur, and was eagerly seized. Louis, a necessary prop to the elaborate structure devised by the wisdom of the deputies, was deliberately made use of. Discredited, a virtual prisoner, finished as a monarch, he was converted into a constitutional fiction, and was compelled by his circumstances to resume the farce of kingship, and to put his signature to the Constitution which, on the 3rd of September, was sent to him.

The Constitution of 1791 was compounded partly of political theory, partly of revolutionary effort, of desire to pull down the prerogatives of the monarchy in favour of the middle class. It was prefaced by a declaration of the rights of man that stamps the whole as a piece of class legislation. By this all Frenchmen were guaranteed certain fundamental rights of justice, of opinion, of speech, of opportunity,—these were passive rights. There were, however, active rights as well; and those were reserved for a privileged class.[1]

[1] There is no opportunity here for discussing adequately the clause in the declaration to the effect that every citizen

Only those paying taxes equivalent to three days' labour had active political rights, that is, the right to vote. In primary and secondary assemblies they were to elect the 750 deputies who were to constitute the sole representative chamber. This chamber was to sit for two years, the King having no authority to dissolve or prorogue it; and it was to possess full legislative power subject to the King's suspensive veto.

The King was chief executive official, with a large power of appointment, and general control of matters of foreign policy. He was not to choose his ministers from among the deputies, and he lost all direct administrative control in the local sense. The intendants, and the provinces, and the généralités were gone; instead of them was a new territorial division into departments, in which local elective self-government was established. Communes and departments were to choose their own govern-

is entitled to concur in making laws. That clause apparently conflicts with what I have said above. My explanation of the discrepancy is based on this: that the declaration is a much tinkered, composite document, made up over a period of many months, and not logical at every point. The clause here mentioned I explain as a direct echo of the elections to the States-General; it was one of the first drafted; its precise significance was soon lost sight of and its inconsistency remained unnoticed.

ing committees, and the old centralized administration of the Bourbons had for the moment to make way for an opposite conception of government.

The signing of the constitution by the King brought it into effect, and thereby an election became necessary for constituting the new representative body, a body that was to be known as the *Législative*. Before leaving its parent body, however, that began as States-General, became a national assembly and was later known as the *Constituante*, a word or two may be added to emphasize points not yet sufficiently indicated. The assembly changed in opinion and attitude during the course of its history, and was vastly different in September 1791 from what it had been in May 1789. It did achieve the purpose of translating a large part of the demands of the cahiers into legislative enactments; yet it did not learn the meaning of the word toleration, and it did not pave the way for liberty, but only for a doctrine of liberty.

The elections to the *Législative* took place in September, under the influence of several cross currents of opinion. There was a slight reaction among certain classes in Paris in favour of the King, and several demonstrations took place which an abler and more active monarch might have turned to advantage. On the other hand, the Jacobin Club attempted to use its machinery to influence the action of the electoral meetings. As a result, when the deputies met on the 1st of October, it was calculated that about 400 belonged to the floating central mass, 136 to the Jacobins, that is, Jacobins in the new Robespierre-Danton sense, 264 to the *Feuillants*. Among the latter there was a general inclination towards a policy of rehabilitating the royal power.

The personnel of the new assembly differed totally from that of its predecessor, because of a self-denying ordinance whereby the members of the *Constituante* had excluded themselves from the new assembly. Yet there were many notable men among the new deputies, nearly all, however, Jacobins:—Brissot, the journalist, soon to be leader of a wing of the party that detaches itself from the one that follows Robespierre; Vergniaud, great as an orator; Isnard, Guadet, Gensonné; Condorcet, marquis and mathematician, philosopher, physicist and republican, noble mind and practical thinker; Cambon, stalwart in politics as in finance; Couthon, hostile to Brissot, later to be one of the Robespierre triumvirate.

This Jacobin group nearly at once established its influence over the more flaccid part of the assembly. Through its club organization it packed the public galleries of the house, and from that point directed the current of opinion by the judicious application of applause or disapproval. This was reinforced by the *appel nominal,* the manner of voting whereby each individual deputy could be compelled to enter the speaker's rostrum and there declare and explain his vote.

To check the efforts of this dominating party, there was little but the inertia of the Court, and what the *Feuillants* might accomplish. Bailly, La Fayette, Lameth, La Rochefoucauld Liancourt, Clermont Tonnerre were among the conspicuous men of the club, but whatever their worth most of them were associated with a too narrow, unyielding attitude to obtain any wide support. The popular force was not behind them, but, for the moment, behind the Jacobins, and the instant the Jacobins became engaged in a struggle against the *Feuillants,* it pushed against the latter and presently toppled them over. Had the *Feuillants* and the Court come together, there was yet a chance that the tide would be stemmed. But that proved impossible. To the royal family foreign help, foreign intervention, appeared the only chance of relief, and Marie Antoinette had long been urging her brother Leopold to come to her assistance. No course could have been more fatal, and the more probable intervention became, the more the democratic party appeared a patriotic party, and the more the King and Queen seemed traitors to the national cause.

It was the foreign question that immediately engrossed the chief attention of the *Législative,* and the foreign question always led back to the great internal one represented by the King. At Coblenz, in the dominions of the Archbishop of Trier, the Comte de Provence had set up what was virtually a government of his own. The *émigrés* had 3,000 or 4,000 men under arms, and a royal council organized, all that was necessary to administer France if she could be regained. The Législative now aimed a blow at them; the *émigrés* were to return to France before the 1st of January 1792, and those failing to do this were to be punishable by death. The decree was sent to the King who, unwilling to sign assent to the death of his brother and nobles, used his constitutional right of veto.

This was the beginning of a conflict between

the assembly and the King, a struggle that showed the determination of the former not to recognise the right of veto prescribed by the Constitution. The *Législative* followed its attack on the *émigrés* by one on the priests. The clergy was discontented and, in the west, showed signs of inciting the peasantry to revolt; it was therefore decreed that every member of the clergy might be called on to take the oath to the civil constitution. This, again, the King vetoed, encouraged in his attitude by the *Feuillants*. The old struggle was being renewed; Jacobins and *Feuillants* were fighting one another over the person of the King.

There was one question, however, on which the *Feuillants* and Brissot's wing of the Jacobins agreed; both wanted war. La Fayette, chief figure among the *Feuillants,* had sunk rapidly in popularity since his repression of the mob in July. In October he had resigned his command of the national guard. In November he had been defeated by the Jacobin Pétion for the mayoralty of Paris. He now hoped for a military command, and saw in war the opportunity for consolidating a victorious army by means of which the King and Constitution might be imposed on Paris.

Brissot, ambitious and self-confident, his

head turned at the prospect of a conflagration, saw in a European war a field large enough in which to develop his untried statesmanship. The pretexts for war lay ready to hand. There was not only the tense situation arising between Austria and France because of the relation between the two reigning families, but there was also acute friction over certain territories belonging to German sovereign princes, such as those of Salm or Montbéliard, that were enclaved within the French border. Could the extinction of the feudal rights hold over such territory as German princes held within the borders of France? Such was the vexatious question which those princes were carrying to their supreme tribunal, that of the Emperor at Vienna.

The opposition to the war was not so weighty. Louis realized the danger clearly enough, and knew that Austrian success would be visited on his head. Yet he was so helpless that he had to call the *Feuillant* nominee, Count Louis de Narbonne, his own natural cousin, to the ministry of war. The King was not alone in his opposition to the war,—Robespierre and Marat, nearly in accord, both stood for peace. Robespierre, from the first, had foreseen the course of the Revolution, had prophetically feared the success of some soldier of fortune,—he was at this moment that unknown lieutenant of artillery, Napoleone Buonaparte, —who should with a stroke of the sword convert the Revolution to his purposes. Marat, in his more hectic, malevolent, uncertain way, was haunted by the same presentiment, and what he saw in war was this: "What afflicts the friends of liberty is that we have more to fear from success than from defeat . . . the danger is lest one of our generals be crowned with victory and lest . . . he lead his victorious army against the capital to secure the triumph of the Despot. I invoke heaven that we may meet with constant defeat . . . and that our soldiers . . . drown their leaders in their own blood."—This Marat wrote on the 24th of April 1792, in his little pamphlet newspaper *l' Ami du peuple*.

During the first part of 1792 the popular agitation grew. France was now throwing all the enthusiasm, the vital emotion of patriotism into her internal upheaval. Rouget de Lisle invented his great patriotic hymn, christened in the following August the *Marseillaise*. Men who could get no guns, armed themselves with pikes. The red Phrygian cap of liberty was adopted. The magic word, citizen, became the cherished appellation of the multitude. And in the assembly the orators declaimed vehemently against the traitors, the supporters of the foreigner in their midst. Vergniaud, from the tribune of the assembly menacing the Austrian princess of the Tuileries, exclaimed: "Through this window I perceive the palace where perfidious counsels delude the Sovereign. . . . Terror and panic have often issued from its portals; this day I bid them re-enter, in the name of the Law; let all its inmates know that it is the King alone who is inviolable, that the Law will strike the guilty without distinction, and that no head on which guilt reposes can escape its sword."

The thunders of Vergniaud and the other Jacobin orators rolled not in vain. By March the Brissotins dominated the situation. They frightened the King into acquiescence in their war policy and they drove Narbonne and the Fayettists, their temporary allies, from office, installing a new ministry made up of their own adherents. That new ministry included Roland, Clavière and Dumouriez;—Roland, a hard-headed, hard-working man of business, whose young wife with her beauty and enthusiasm was to be the soul of the unfortunate Girondin party; Clavière, a banker, speculator, friend of Mirabeau, and generally doubtful liberal; Dumouriez, a soldier, able, adventurous, of large instincts political and human, ambitious and forceful beyond his colleagues.

The Brissotin ministry was well equipped with talent, and was intended to carry through the war, which was voted by the assembly on the 20th of April. This step had been gradually led up to by an acrimonious exchange of diplomatic votes. The war, now that it had broken out, was found to involve more powers than Austria. The king of Prussia, unwilling to let Austria pose as the sole defender of the Germanic princes of the Rhineland, had in August 1791 joined the Emperor in the declaration of Pillnitz, threatening France with coercion. He now acted up to this, and joined in the war as the ally of the Emperor. Leopold died in March, and was succeeded by his son, Marie Antoinette's nephew, Francis II.

Three armies were formed by France for the conflict, and were placed under the orders of Rochambeau, La Fayette, and Luckner. They were weak in numbers, as the fortresses soaked up many thousands of men, and unprepared for war. The allies concentrated their troops in the neighbourhood of Coblenz. The

Duke of Brunswick was placed in command, and by the end of July perfected arrangements for marching on Paris with an Austro-Prussian army of 80,000 men.

The breaking out of war inflamed still further the political excitement of France. In April a festival, or demonstration, was held in honour of the soldiers of Chateauvieux' Swiss regiment, now released from the galleys. Angry protests arose from the moderates, an echo of the assembly's vote of thanks to Bouillé for repressing the mutineers six months before. These protests, however, went unheeded, for the Jacobins were now virtually masters of Paris. Not only did they control the public galleries of the assembly but they had gained a majority on the Commune and had secured for Manuel and Danton its legal executive offices of *procureur* and *substitut*.

In May difficulties arose between the King and his ministers, arising partly from the exercise of the power of veto once more. On the 12th of June the ministers were forced from office and were replaced by moderates or Fayettists, Dumouriez going to the army to replace Rochambeau. The Brissotin party, furious at this defeat, decided on a monster demonstration against the King for the 20th of June.

The 20th of June 1792 was one of the great days of the Revolution, but, on the whole, less an insurrection than a demonstration. Out of the two great faubourgs of the working classes, St. Antoine and St. Marceaux, came processions of market porters, market women, coal heavers, workmen, citizens, with detachments of national guards here and there. Santerre, a popular brewer and national guard commander, appeared the leader; but the procession showed little sign of having recourse to violence. Bouquets were carried, and banners with various inscriptions such as: "We want union!" "Liberty!" One of the most extreme said: "Warning to Louis XVI: the people, weary of suffering, demand liberty or death!"

Proceeding to the assembly a petition was tumultuously presented wherein it was declared that the King must observe the law, and that if he was responsible for the continued inactivity of the armies he must go. The mob then flowed on to the palace, was brought up by some loyal battalions of national guards; but presently forced one of the gates and irresistibly poured in. A disorderly scene followed.

The King maintained his coolness and dignity. For four long hours the mob pushed through the palace, jostling, apostrophising, the King and Queen. A few national guards, a few members of the assembly, attempted to give Louis some sort of protection. But he was practically surrounded and helpless. What saved him was his coolness, his good sense, and the fact that there was no intent to do him bodily harm save among some groups too unimportant to make themselves felt. To please the men of the faubourgs Louis consented to place a red liberty cap on his head, and to empty a bottle of wine as a sign of fraternization. Finally Vergniaud and Pétion succeeded in having the palace evacuated; and the assassination of Louis, which many had feared and a few hoped, had been averted.

CHAPTER X

THE MASSACRES

THE event of the 20th of June was like lightning flashing in darkness. Instantly people saw where they were. Moderate, loyal, reasonable men, startled at the danger of the King, smarting at the indignity he had suffered, fearful of mob rule and mob violence, rallied to the throne, signed petitions protesting against the event. Louis himself, realizing that his life was in jeopardy, made appeals both to the assembly and to his people.

The first reply to the King's appeal, unsolicited and unappreciated, came from La Fayette. On receiving news of the event of the 20th he left his headquarters and reached Paris on the 28th. He appealed to the assembly and rallied the centre, still responsive if a leader could be found. He then began to concert measures for getting control of the city by means of the national guards. At this point, however, his scheme failed. The Court would not support him, the King too prudent, the Queen too impolitic. Marie Antoinette herself, it is said, in her rancorous dislike of La Fayette, gave Pétion the secret as to his contemplated use of the national guards; and this proved fatal. Checked by the action of the mayor and the Jacobins, unsupported by the Tuileries, La Fayette had to abandon his efforts.

Another attempt followed. The Department of the Seine, presided by La Rochefoucauld, tried to assert its constitutional authority over the great city situated within its limits. It voted the suspension of Pétion, mayor of Paris, and of Manuel, his procureur, for dereliction of duty in failing to maintain order on the 20th of June.

The action of La Rochefoucauld in suspending Pétion took place on the 7th of July, a moment at which the advance of the Duke of Brunswick was momentarily expected and at which the national excitement was tending to overpower the royalist reaction. This reaction was now checked. The Jacobins were resolved to use mob pressure to whatever extent was necessary for accomplishing their purpose. On the 11th they passed through the assembly a declaration that the country was in danger, and two days later imposed a vote quashing the action of the Department and reinstating Pétion.

The ferment now blended inextricably the war fever and the action against the King. Volunteers were enrolling for the army. National guards were being summoned from the provinces to renew the federation of 1791, and the violent section of the agitators saw in these national guards the means for pushing over the royal authority. A demonstration better organized than that of the 20th of June, and armed, could rid France of the Bourbon incubus. Preparations for such a demonstration were at once taken in hand.

Among the provincial troops now assembled in or marching towards Paris, there was no body more remarkable than the battalion of the 300 Marseillais. Like a whirlwind of patriotic emotion they swept through France, dragging the cannon with which they meant to knock at the gates of the Tuileries, chanting Rouget's new song forever to be associated with the name of their own city. These Marseillais were red-hot republicans, and in judging the political situation of that moment this constitutes one of the salient points. The Parisian patriots were on the whole far less republican than those of the provinces.

Among the men who were organizing the new demonstration the greater part meant nothing more than ridding themselves of Louis, of an executive officer whom they regarded as treacherous and as secretly in league with the enemy. What should come after him they did not much consider. In the forming of this state of opinion the individual action of Robespierre had played a great part. Robespierre, who feared in war the opportunity for the soldier, saw in republicanism merely the triumph of a Cromwell; to him La Fayette was a tangible danger, the word *republic* an empty formula. And so, with an influence still widening, despite his opposition to the war, he steadily preached the doctrine that the form of government was nothing so long as civil, social and political equality were secured.

At the parade held on the 14th of July,—the Marseillais had not yet arrived,—there were no cries of *Vive le roi,* and none of, *Vive la république,* but *Vive la nation* was the adopted formula. Yet at the same moment Billaud-Varennes, one of the most advanced of the Jacobins, was addressing the Club in favour of a republic; and the *fédérés* formed a central committee which on the 17th petitioned the assembly for the suspension of the King. To support the movement further the section committees were decreed in continuous session, and came under the control of the organization.

On the 30th of July, Brunswick crossed the frontier; the advance of his columns was heralded by a proclamation or manifesto. In this document he announced to the people of France that he entered the country as the ally of their sovereign, and with the purpose of visiting on Paris an "exemplary and never-to-be-forgotten vengeance . . . military execution and total subversion," and of bringing "the guilty rebels to the death they have deserved." Copies of the manifesto reached Paris on the 3rd of August, with immediate effect. To Louis the Prussian general's utterances appeared so incredible that they were promptly disavowed as a forgery. To the people they confirmed the suspicion that had been rankling for three long years, that had been envenomed by all the poison of Marat. A howl of execration arose, a howl not against Brunswick but against the inmates of the Tuileries; and in that howl the voices of the Marseillais, who had just reached the city, were raised loudest.

The inevitable result followed in just one week, a week spent in preparations by the popular leaders. At one o'clock in the morning of the 10th of August delegates from the sections met at the Hotel de Ville and assumed control of the city. This body was joined by Danton, Marat and Hébert, among others, and of these Danton more than anyone else represented the driving power. Orders were given for ringing the tocsin. All Paris knew the movement was coming, and understood the signal.

At the Tuileries preparations for resistance had been made. The Marquis de Mandat took charge of the defence. He had about 1,500 well-disposed national guards from the western or middle class districts, and about 1,000 excellent Swiss infantry of the King's household troops. These he posted to good advantage, guarding the palace and the bridges over the Seine to the south. For a while all went well. The insurrection began slowly; and when it did roll up as far as the bridges Mandat's musketry held it easily at bay.

The insurrectional Commune now realized that Mandat was a considerable obstacle and set to work to remove him. In his official station as a national guard commander he was under the jurisdiction of the mayor, so Pétion was made to write, ordering him to report at the Hotel de Ville. Mandat declined to obey. The attack still hung fire. The order was repeated. Mandat, this time, weakly allowed himself to be persuaded into compliance. He proceeded to the Hotel de Ville,—and was butchered on the stairs by a band of insurgents.

After the defence had lost its general, and with daylight over the scene, events moved fast. The national guards at the palace could not be kept to their posts in the absence of their chief and in presence of the swelling numbers of the attackers. The defence of the bridges had to be given up and the Swiss withdrew into the palace. A lull followed while the insurrection gathered up its strength for the attack on the Tuileries itself.

During that lull, at half past eight, Louis, with his family, left the palace. He believed resistance useless; he feared a massacre might occur; he was averse as ever to bloodshed; and so was persuaded that his best course would be to seek refuge in the assembly.

Just as Louis left, the real attack was delivered on the palace. The Swiss replied with musketry, sallied out, charged the insurgents and drove them across the Carrousel; then they returned, and presently received a written order from the King bidding them not to fire. This momentarily paralyzed the defence. The insurgents, led by the provincial *fédérés,* were not yet beaten, but flowed back once more to the attack. Some field pieces which they had, breached the palace doors, a sharp struggle followed, and soon the insurgents had got a foothold. What followed was a massacre. Many of the Swiss were cut down in the corridors and rooms of the palace. Others were mown down by musketry trying to escape across the Tuileries gardens. A few got away and sought refuge in a near-by church, but were there overtaken by the popular fury, and butchered. The rage of the people was unbridled, and success turned it into ferocity, even bestiality. The bodies of the Swiss were mutilated in an atrocious fashion.

While the triumphant insurgents were sacking the palace and committing their barbarities on the unfortunate Swiss, Louis and his family remained unmolested in the assembly. They were to remain there for three days while their fate was being decided, temporary accommodation being found for them. The situation was really this, that no party was yet quite prepared for the destruction of the King himself, only of the royal power. The assembly which, a year earlier, had assumed the position that the King was necessary to the constitution had now virtually abandoned it, and the Commune, while going much further than the assembly, was not yet ready to strike Louis. But it did claim the custody of the royal family, and that, after a three days' struggle, the assembly conceded. On the 13th of August the royal family went to imprisonment in the Temple, a small mediæval dungeon in the central quarter of Paris.

Only about three hundred members of the assembly were present to face the storm when Louis sought refuge in its midst. Vergniaud was president. Presently the Commune sent a request that the assembly should depose the King. Vergniaud thereupon proposed a middle course; the assembly could suspend the King from his functions and call together a convention to solve the constitutional question that the suspension of the Executive presented; in the meanwhile ministers elected by the assembly should constitute a provisional Executive Council. These proposals were carried, and the Executive Council was elected; it contained most of the members of the

Brissotin ministry, but with a new member. At the head of the poll was Danton, and Danton was made Minister of Justice.

Danton now clearly appears as the man of the situation. The people had triumphed, and Danton was the statesman of the people. He bridged the gap between the Commune and the assembly. He gave rein to the popular fury and to the destruction of every anti-popular influence, and he attempted, by placing himself at the head of the flood, to direct it against the great external danger that menaced France.

On the 11th of August the assembly decreed that universal suffrage should be put in force for the elections to the convention. Large police powers were voted to the Commune, which Robespierre now joined; and laws were passed aimed against those suspected of being in sympathy with the advancing army or with Louis. The *appel nominal* was placed in force in many of the sections, and Danton put the machinery of his ministry at work to reinforce these measures, to convert them to use for terrorizing the moderates, for satisfying the popular suspicions against the aristocrats, for weighing on the elections. The primaries were to begin on the 27th of August, those for Paris on the 2d of September; the meeting of electors for nominating the deputies of Paris was to take place on the 5th of September.

Meanwhile Brunswick's columns were making steady, methodical progress through the hills of Lorraine, through the frontier belt of fortresses. The French armies in their front were weak in numbers, even weaker in leadership. La Fayette, who had attempted to reaffirm the constitution on hearing of the event of the 10th of August, deemed it prudent to ride over the frontier when commissioners of the assembly reached his camp; he was seized as a prisoner by the allies to remain their captive for many years. On the 20th the Prussian guns opened on Longwy; on the 23rd it surrendered. On the 30th the siege of Verdun was begun, Verdun which Louis had so nearly reached the year before. It was generally known that the fortress could not stand more than a few days. Between it and Paris there was only the Argonne, a few miles of hilly passes, and then 100 miles of open country.

The steady advance of Brunswick drove Paris into a state approaching delirium. On the news of the fall of Longwy reaching the city, the extremists, their appetites whetted by the butchery of the Swiss, began to plot a massacre of the political prisoners, of the royalists, of the suspect. On the 28th of August Danton, riding on the wings of the storm, asked power from the Commune to carry out domiciliary visits for the purpose of arresting suspects. This power was granted, and in three days the prisons were filled to overflowing, priests and persons of title being specially singled out for arrest.

By the 1st of September Paris was ready to answer the Duke of Brunswick, was ready for the stroke that was to destroy the anti-revolutionists, that was to strike terror to the hearts of all enemies of the people. But the awfulness of the deed delayed its execution. The day passed in high-wrought excitement; at any moment news might arrive of the fall of Verdun,—that might be the signal for the explosion of the popular fury.

On the 2d there was still no news of Verdun, but the moment could not be delayed much longer. In the night preparations had been made. Men to do the business of popular execution had been approached; some had been offered pay. The leaders were determined to carry through their enterprise. In the assembly Danton thundered from the tribune:

"Verdun has not yet surrendered. One part of the people will march to the frontier, another will throw up intrenchments, and the rest will defend our cities with pikes. Paris will second these great efforts. The assembly will become a war committee. We demand that whoever refuses to serve shall be punished by death. The tocsin you will hear presently is not a signal of alarm; it is ringing the charge against the enemies of our country. To conquer them we must be audacious, yet more audacious, and still more audacious, and France is saved."

The tocsin rang, as Danton had ordered; alarm guns were fired; drummers woke the echoes of the streets and of the squares, and presently the deed of supreme audacity and of supreme horror began to come into being. Crowds collected about the prisons. Groups forced a way in. More or less improvised committees took possession, and massacre began.

The massacre of September is one of the most lurid events of the Revolution, easier therefore for the romancist to deal with than for the historian. Its horrors are quite beyond question. At one point, Bicêtre, the killing continued until late on the 6th, nearly four days. The total number of victims was very large, possibly between 2,000 and 3,000. At many places the slaughter was indiscriminate, accompanied by nameless barbarities, carried out by gangs of brutal ruffians who were soon intoxicated with gore and with wine. But alongside of these aspects were others more difficult to do justice to, but the careful weighing of which is necessary if any just estimate of the event is to be reached.

The massacring was carried out by a small number of individuals, perhaps two or three hundred in all, and of these a considerable proportion undoubtedly acted in a spirit of blind political and social rage, and in the belief that they were carrying out an act of justice. A large mass of citizens gave the massacres their approval by forming crowds about the prison doors. As to these crowds there are two salient facts. The first is that on the first day they were large and excited, and afforded that moral support without which the massacres could hardly have been carried out. After the first day they diminished rapidly; and by the end of the third day all popular support was gone, and a feeling of horror had seized on the city and supplanted everything else. Then again the mob, as it crowded about the prison doors, showed a marked attitude. Many of the prisoners, those who were so lucky as to pass for good citizens and friends of the people, were released. As these came out the crowd received them with every sign of joy and of fraternization. When on the contrary it was a victim coming out to be slaughtered, there was silence, no shouting, no exultation.

In other words, the event was, with most, an act of popular justice, and this was the appearance it had even when seen from the interior of the prisons. At l'Abbaye Maillard presided over the self-appointed tribunal, and it is impossible to doubt that, whenever he was satisfied that the prisoner deserved his freedom, he attempted to secure his life. The case of St. Méard, an aristocrat, a colonel, who had enough good sense and courage to speak plainly to the judges, avowing himself a royalist but persuading them that he took no part in anti-revolutionary schemes, is most illuminating. Maillard declared he saw no harm in him; he was acquitted; and was fraternally embraced by the crowd when he safely passed the fatal door.

All did not have the good fortune of St Méard. The case of the Princesse de Lamballe, at La Force, must serve to give the worst side of, and to close, this chapter of blood. Long the friend, confidante and agent of the Queen, she had followed her to the Temple, and had been removed from there but a few days previously. She was too well known and too near Marie Antoinette to have any chance of escape. In a fainting condition she was dragged before the tribunal, and was soon passed out to the executioners. It is not probable that she had much consciousness of what followed. The gang of murderers at this point were butchers of the Halles, and they apparently treated their victim as they might have a beast brought to the slaughter. She was carried under the arms to where a pile of bodies had accumulated, and, in a moment made ready, was butchered in the technical sense of the term. Her head was hoisted on a pike, as also other parts of her dismembered anatomy, and carried in triumph to be displayed under the windows of the prisoners at the Temple.

Verdun fell on the 2d of September, at the very moment when Danton was announcing its continued resistance. On the 5th the Duke of Brunswick resumed his march on Paris, and on the same day, the electors of that city met and chose twenty deputies to the convention; their choice was coloured by the fact that the massacres were still continuing. At the head of the poll stood Robespierre; Danton was next; among the others may be noted Camille Desmoulins, Marat, and, last of all, the duc d'Orléans, who a few days later metamorphosed his Bourbon name into Philippe *Egalité*.

Throughout France the electoral process was everywhere giving much the same result. Less than one-tenth of the electors used their franchise; and the extreme party won great successes. By the middle of September the new deputies were reaching Paris. The *Législative* in its last moments was feeble and undignified. Marat threatened it with massacre, and declared that its members were as much the enemies of the country as were the imprisoned aristocrats. Under this menace the Législative watched the massacres of September without raising a hand to protect its unfortunate victims. Danton did the same. As minister of Justice the prisoners and the tribunals were under his special charge. But although he may have facilitated the escape of some individuals, and although he took no direct part, yet he believed that no government could be established strong enough to save the Revolution, at such a crisis as it had reached, save by paying this toll of blood to the suspicion, the vengeance, the cruelty, the justice of the people. He dared to pay the price, and later he, and he alone, dared to shoulder the responsibility.

CHAPTER XI

ENDING THE MONARCHY

ON the 20th and 21st of September 1792 the Convention met, the Bourbon monarchy fell, and the Duke of Brunswick was defeated, a coincidence of memorable events.

Brunswick, pushing on from Verdun into the defiles of the Argonne, had two armies operating against him, trying to stop his march; the one under Dumouriez, the other under Kellermann. He forced a way, however, but at the further side, about the hills of Valmy, had to face the combined armies of his adversaries. Brunswick was now much reduced by sickness, and was much worried over supplies and his lengthening line of communications. In a faint-hearted way he deployed for attack. Dumouriez for the moment checked him by a skillful disposition of his superior artillery. But if the superbly drilled Prussian infantry were sent forward it seemed as though the result could not be long in doubt.

Brunswick methodically and slowly made his preparations for the attack, but just at the moment when it should have been delivered, Dumouriez, divining his opponent's hesitation, imposed on him. Riding along the French front with his staff he placed his hat on the point of his sword and rode forward, singing the Marseillaise. His whole army catching the refrain advanced towards the enemy; and Brunswick at once took up a defensive attitude, which he maintained till the close of the battle. The unsteady battalions and half-drilled volunteers of Dumouriez had suddenly revealed the fact that they were a national army, and that they possessed the most formidable of military weapons, patriotism. That was an innovation in 18th-century warfare, an innovation that was to result in some notable triumphs. At Valmy it led to the Prussians retiring from a battle field on which they had left only a few score of dead. Soon afterwards Brunswick began a retreat that was to lead him back to the Rhine.

On the day after Valmy, the Convention assembled. The extreme Jacobins, soon to be known from their seats in the assembly as the Mountain, numbered about fifty. Danton and

Robespierre were the two most conspicuous; among their immediate supporters not hitherto mentioned may be noted Carnot, Fouché, Tallien, and St. Just. A much larger group, of which the moderate Jacobins formed the backbone, were inclined to look to Brissot for leadership and are generally described as Girondins. This name came from the small group of the deputies of the Gironde, that represented perhaps better than any other, the best force of provincial liberalism but at the same time a revolt against terrorism, massacre and the supremacy of Paris. Within the last sixty years, however, the term Girondin has come into use as a label for all those positive political elements in the Convention that attempted a struggle against the Mountain for leadership and against Paris for moderate and national government. Among the Girondins may be noted Brissot, Vergniaud, Condorcet, and the Anglo-American veteran of republicanism, Tom Paine. Between the Mountain and the Gironde sat the Plaine, or the Marais, as it was called, that non-committal section of the house strongest in numbers but weakest in moral courage, where sat such men as Barras, Barère, Cambon, Grégoire, Lanjuinais,

Sieyès. These were the men who mostly drifted, and, as the Mountain triumphed, threw into it many more or less sincere recruits.

The first business of the new assembly was pressing; it did not comport much variation of opinion. The constitutional question must be settled; and so a vote, immediately taken, pronounced the fall of the monarchy. Even at this moment, however, there was no enthusiasm for a republic and there was no formal pronouncement that France accepted that régime. Yet in fact she had; and on the following day the Convention, in further decrees, assumed the existence of the Republic to be an established fact.

There was a question, however, even more burning, because more debatable, than the fall of the monarchy; and this was the massacres, and beyond the massacres, the policy of the party that had accepted them. The great majority of the deputies on arriving in Paris from the provinces had been horror-struck. Lanjuinais said: "When I arrived in Paris, I shuddered!" Brissot and the Girondins put that feeling of the assembly behind their policy. They adopted an attitude of uncompromising condemnation towards the men of September, and attempted to wrest their influence from them. To accomplish this they had among other things to outbid their rivals for popular support, and so it happened that many of them who were at heart constitutional monarchists adopted a strong republican attitude which went beyond their real convictions.

The Girondins attacked at once. The conduct of the Commune, of the sectional committees was impugned. Marat, on taking his seat, was subjected to a furious onslaught that nearly ended in actual violence. But he packed the galleries with his supporters, retorted bitterly in the *Ami du peuple,* and succeeded in weathering the storm. But the Convention agreed that a committee of six should investigate, and that a guard of 4,500 men should be drawn from the departments for the protection of the Convention. This was a worthy beginning, but it ended, as it began, in words. Paris answered the Girondins with deeds.

The proposed bringing in of an armed force from the departments stirred Paris to fury once more. Brissot was expelled from the Jacobin Club. Many of the sections presented petitions protesting against the departmental guard. But for a while the moderates held their ground, even appeared to gain a little. Addresses kept reaching the assembly from the departments protesting against the domination of Paris. Small detachments of loyal national guards arrived in the city; and in November, on an election being held for the mayoralty of Paris, although very few voters went to the polls, the Jacobins failed to carry their candidate. It was to be their last defeat before the 9th of Thermidor.

It was at this moment that took place the famous iron chest incident. A safe was discovered and broken open during the perquisitions made in the palace of the Tuileries. Roland placed in the custody of the house a packet of papers found in this safe, and among these papers were accounts showing the sums paid to Mirabeau, and to other members of the assembly, by the Court. There resulted much abuse of Mirabeau, whose body was removed from the Pantheon where it had been ceremoniously interred, and also much political pressure on deputies who either were or feared to be incriminated.

A number of the young Girondins were now meeting constantly at Madame Roland's, and their detestation of the Mountain was heightened and idealized by the enthusiasms of their charming hostess. Louvet, brilliant, ambitious, hot-headed, threw himself into the conflict, and, on the 29th of October, launched a tremendous philippic against Robespierre. As oratory it was successful, but it failed in political effect. After their ill success against Marat, the Girondins stood no chance of success against Robespierre unless their words led to immediate action, unless their party was solid and organized, unless they had some means of obtaining a practical result. In all this they failed. Robespierre obtained a delay to prepare his reply, and then a careful speech and packed galleries triumphed over Louvet's ill-judged attack.

The Mountain had survived the first storms. It was soon able to use the question of the King as a means of distracting attention from the massacres, and of giving the party a ground on which it might hope to meet the Gironde on more even terms. For any attempt at moderation on the part of the Girondins could be met with the charge of veiled royalism, of anti-patriotism, and such a charge at that moment was the most damning that a party or an individual could incur.

The Convention, having agreed that it would consider the question of Louis, and having appointed a committee to that end, heard the report of its committee on the 3rd of November. From this it appeared that there were numerous charges that could be preferred against Louis; but what was the tribunal before which such charges could be tried? There could be but one answer. Only the people of France could judge Louis, and the Convention stood for the people. Lengthy debates followed on these questions, and the speech of Robespierre, a speech in which he stood nearly alone in taking a logical view of the situation, was perhaps its most remarkable product. Robespierre said: "The assembly has been drawn off on side issues. There is no question here of a legal action. Louis is not an accused person; you are not judges,—you are only representatives of the nation. It is not for you to render judgment, but to take a measure of national security. . . . Louis was king, and the republic has come into existence; the wonderful question you are debating is resolved by these words. Louis was dethroned for his crimes; Louis denounced the people of France as rebels; he called to chastise them the armies of his brother tyrants to his help; victory and the people have decided that he alone is the rebel; Louis therefore cannot be judged because he has been judged. He stands condemned, or if not, then the republic stands not acquitted. . . . For if Louis can be the subject of an action, Louis may be pronounced guiltless. . . . A people does not judge after the manner of a judicial body; it does not render sentence, it launches the thunderbolt."

On the same day, the 3rd of December, without accepting Robespierre's point of view, the Convention voted that the King should be brought to trial. The Gironde, feeling the current now drawing them fast to a catastrophe, attempted, in feeble fashion, to change its direction, urging that an appeal should be made to the country. This failed, and a week later Louis was brought before the assembly.

The royal family had been kept in very strict confinement at the Temple. The Commune officials in whose charge they were placed were for the most part men of the lower classes, brutal, arrogant, suspicious, and somewhat oppressed with responsibility and the fear of possible attempts at a rescue. In these conditions the royal family suffered severely, and, under suffering, rapidly began to regain some of the ground they had lost while fortune smiled. Against insult the royal dignity asserted itself, and in adversity the simplicity and kindliness of Louis began rather suddenly to look like something not so very remote from saintliness; such is the relation of surroundings and background to the effect produced by a man's life and character.

Before the Convention, on the 11th of December, Louis, mild and dignified, listened in some bewilderment to a long list of so-called charges, of which the most salient accused him of complicity with Bouillé in a plot against his subjects, and of having broken his oath to the constitution. When asked what answer he had to make, he denied the charges, and demanded time to prepare a defence and to obtain legal assistance. This was granted, and an adjournment was taken. From all of which it appears that Louis accepted the false ground which the Convention had marked out for him, and lacked the logical sense of Robespierre.

During the adjournment, which was for two weeks, the Girondins made one more attempt to dodge the issue, to refer the trial of the King to the electorate. Behind them was a great mass of opinion. The department of Finisterre passed resolutions demanding the suspension of Marat, Robespierre and Danton; it approached the neighbouring departments with a view to combining their armed forces and sending them to Paris. Even with such demonstrations to strengthen their hands the Girondins were in too false a position, were too much orators and not men of action, to save themselves; Paris held them inexorably to their detested task.

On the 26th, the trial was resumed, and, save for judgment, concluded. Louis was in charge of Santerre, commanding the national guard of Paris. His advocates, Malesherbes, Tronchet and de Sèze, did their duty with courage and ability, after which the King was removed, and the Convention resolved itself into a disorderly and clamorous meeting in which the public galleries added as much to the din as the members themselves.

More debates followed, of which the turn was reached on the 3rd of January. On that day Barère, most astute of those who sat in the centre, keenest to detect the tremor of the straw that showed which way public passion was about to blow, ascended the tribune and delivered his opinion. Anxiously the house hung on the words of the oracle of moral cowardice, and heard that oracle pronounce the destruction of the King as a measure of public safety. From that moment all attempts to save him were in vain.

The Girondins did not confine themselves to numerous efforts to displace the responsibility of judging from the Convention to the people. Three days after Barère's speech Dumouriez arrived in Paris. As La Fayette had a few months before, so did Dumouriez now, appear to be the man of the sword so dreaded by Robespierre, the successful soldier ready to convert the Revolution to his own profit, or if not to his own to that of his party, the Girondins. During more than two weeks Dumouriez remained in the city, casting about for some means of saving the King, but constantly checked by the Jacobins, who through Pache, minister of war, kept control of the artillery and troops near Paris.

On the 15th of January the Convention came to a vote, amid scenes of intense excitement. Was Louis guilty? And if so what should be his punishment? Six hundred and eighty-three members voted affirmatively to the first question. Three hundred and sixty-one voted the penalty of death. About the same number equivocated in a variety of forms, the most popular proving the one that declared for imprisonment or exile, to be changed to death in case of invasion. Vergniaud, as president, at the end of a session that lasted 36 hours, declared the sentence of the Convention to be death.

On the 19th of January one last effort was made. A motion for a respite was proposed, but was rejected, 380 to 310; and the Convention then fixed the 21st as the day for the King's execution. On that day Louis accordingly went to the scaffold. The guillotine was set up in the great open space known at various epochs as the Place Louis XV, de la Révolution, and de la Concorde. Louis, after a touching farewell from his family, and after confessing whatever he imagined to be his sins, was driven from the Temple to the place of execution; he was dressed in white. The streets were thronged. The national guard was out in force, and when Louis from the platform attempted to speak, Santerre ordered his drums to roll. A moment later the head of King Louis XVI had fallen, and many mourning royalists were vowing loyalty in their hearts to the little boy of eight, imprisoned in the temple, who to them was King Louis XVII.

CHAPTER XII

THE FALL OF THE GIRONDE

THE disappearance of Louis XVI from the scene left the Mountain and the Gironde face to face, to wage their faction fight, a fight to the knife; while France in her armies more nobly maintained her greater struggle on the frontier. There for a while after Valmy all had prospered. Brunswick had fallen back to Coblenz. A French army under the Marquis de Custine had overrun all the Rhineland as far as Mainz. Dumouriez, transferred from the Ardennes to the Belgian frontier, had invaded the Austrian Netherlands. On the 6th of November he won a considerable victory at Jemmappes, and towards the end of December, he controlled most of the province.

The Convention, elated at these successes, issued decrees proclaiming a crusade against the European tyrannies, and announcing the propaganda of the principles of liberty. But in practice the French invasion did not generally produce very edifying results. Generals and troops plundered unmercifully, to make up for the disorganization of their own service and lack of pay, and even the French Government imposed the expenses of the war on the countries that had to support its horrors.

The close of the year 1792 marked a period of success. The opening of 1793, however, saw the pendulum swing back. New enemies gathered about France. Sardinia, whose province of Savoy had been invaded, now had a considerable army in the field. At short intervals after the execution of Louis, England, Holland, Spain, joined the coalition. And the Convention light-heartedly accepted this accumulation of war. To face the storm it appointed in January a committee of general defence of twenty-five members; but Danton alone would have done better than the twenty-five. While the trial of the King proceeded he was casting about for support in the assembly for a constructive policy. He stretched a hand to the Girondins; they refused it; and Danton turned back to the Mountain once more, compelled to choose between two factions the one that was for the moment willing to act with him.

Through February and into March the military situation kept getting worse, and the Mountain made repeated attacks on the Gironde. On the 5th of March news reached Paris that the Austrians had captured Aix-la-Chapelle, and that the French general Miranda had been compelled to abandon his guns and to retire from before Maestricht, which he was besieging. Danton, who was in the north, arranging the annexation of the Netherlands to France, started for Paris at once. On the 14th the capital heard, with amazement and alarm, that the Vendée had risen in arms for God and King Louis XVII.

The Vendée was a large district of France, a great part of the ancient province of Poitou, lying just to the south of the Loire and near the Atlantic Ocean. A great part of the country was cut up by tracts of forest and thick and numerous hedges. The peasants were fairly prosperous, and well-affected to the priests and seigneurs. The latter were mostly resident landlords, holders of small estates, living near and on kindly terms with their peasantry. The priests and nobles had long viewed the Revolution with aversion, an aversion intensified by the proclamation of the Republic and the execution of the King. And when, on the 26th of February, the Convention passed an army ballot law and sent agents to press recruits among the villages of the Vendée, the peasants joined their natural leaders and rose in arms against the Government. The Vendéens were, in their own country, formidable opponents. They had born leaders, men who showed wonderful courage, dash, and loyalty. They prayed before charging an enemy, and on the march or in battle sang hymns, always the most irresistible of battle songs. Their badges were the white flag, the Bourbon lilies, and the cross. For awhile they swept everything before them.

Danton arrived in Paris on the 8th of March. He immediately attempted to reconcile the factions of the assembly, and to persuade its members to turn their wasted vigour into war measures. From neither side did he receive much encouragement. (To his demands for new levies and volunteer regiments, Robespierre replied that the most urgent step was to purify the army of its anti-revolutionary elements. To his proposal that the executive should be strengthened by composing the ministry of members of the Convention, the Girondins opposed their implacable suspicion and hatred.) But Paris had long been working up its hostility to the Gironde; an insurrectional committee had just come into existence that aimed at dealing with them after the fashion in which it had dealt with Louis on the 10th of August; and the Girondins' stand against Danton precipitated the outbreak.

On the 9th of March a premature and imperfectly organized insurrection occurred, directed against the Gironde. The demonstrators marched against the Convention, but were held in check by a few hundred well-affected provincial national guards. On the 10th it became known that Dumouriez was severely pressed by the Austrians and in danger of being cut off. Under the influence of this news, and with the Girondins showing little fight because of the event of the day before, the Convention passed a measure of terrorism; it voted the establishment of a Revolutionary Tribunal to judge "traitors, conspirators, and anti-revolutionists." In vain Buzot and other Girondins pointed out that this meant establishing "a despotism worse than the old." Danton, unquenchably opportunist, supported the measure, and it was carried. Immediately after this he left Paris for the frontier once more.

On the 18th of March Dumouriez was severely defeated at Neerwinden. And now not only was the Vendée in arms, but Lyons, Marseilles, Normandy, appeared on the point of throwing off the yoke of Paris and of the Jacobins; the situation looked well-nigh desperate. A week later the papers published letters of Dumouriez which showed that ever since the trial of the King the Girondin general had been factious, that is, had been as much inclined to turn his arms against Paris as against the Austrians. Danton was now back from the frontier; he and Robespierre were at once elected to the committee of general defence; and that commitee declared itself in continuous session.

Extraordinary measures were now passed in quick succession which, added to the creation of the Revolutionary Tribunal, made up a formidable machinery of terrorism Deputies of the Convention were sent out on mission to superintend the working of the armies and of the internal police. They were given the widest powers,—were virtually made pro-dictators. On the 1st of April was passed a new law of suspects to reinforce the action of the representatives on mission and of the Revolutionary Tribunal. On the 6th of April was created the executive power that Danton urged the need of so pertinaciously; this was the Committee of

Public Safety, a body of nine members of the Convention, acting secretly, directing the ministers, and having general control of the executive functions. The Girondins had to submit to the measure, and their opponents secured control of the Committee. Among its first members were Danton, Cambon, and Barère.

Just as the Committee of Public Safety came into existence the situation on the frontier was getting even worse. On the 4th of April Dumouriez, fearing that the Convention would send him to the Revolutionary Tribunal, made an attempt to turn his army against the Government, and failing, rode over into the Austrian lines. At the same time, Custine was being driven out of Alsace by the Prussians, who, on the 14th of April, laid siege to Mainz.

With the Mountain immensely strengthened by the formation of the Committee of Public Safety, the attack on the Girondins increased in vigour. Robespierre accused them of complicity with Dumouriez in treasonable intentions against the Republic. The Gironde retaliated, and, on the 13th of April, succeeded in rallying a majority of the Convention in a second onslaught against Marat for his incendiary articles. It was decreed that the *Ami du peuple* should be sent to the Revolutionary

Tribunal. It was the last success of the Girondins, and it did not carry them far. The Jacobins closed their ranks against this assault. They had the Commune and the Revolutionary Tribunal under their control. The former body sent a petition to the Convention demanding the exclusion of twenty-two prominent Girondins as enemies of the Revolution; and a few days later the Tribunal absolved Marat of all his sins.

Incidentally to the bitter struggle between the two factions, great questions, social, political, economic, were being debated, though not with great results. They could really all be brought back to the one fundamental question which the course of the Revolution had brought to the surface. What was to be the position of the poor man, and especially of the poor man in the modern city and under industrial surroundings,—what was to be his position in the new form of social adjustment which the Revolution was bringing about? What about the price of food? the monopoly of capital? the private ownership of property? Such were some of the questions that underlay the debates of the Convention in the spring of 1793.

The food question was dealt with in various

ways. The famous law of the Maximum, passed on the 3rd of May, attempted to regulate the prices of food by a sliding scale tariff. The measure was economically unsound, and in many ways worked injustice; it alarmed property holders and alienated them from the Government. On its own initiative the Commune made great efforts, and with some success, to maintain the food supply of the city, and to keep down the price of bread. Spending about 12,000 francs a day, less than half a sou per head, it succeeded for the most part in keeping bread down to about 3 sous per pound.

But by virtue of what theory of government were the poor entitled to this special protection? Was the Jacobin party prepared to advance towards a socialist or collectivist form of government? Of that there was no sign; and several years were yet to pass before Babeuf was to give weight to a collectivist theory of the State. There were special reasons of some force to explain why the Convention, however much it might be addicted to humanitarian theories, however anxious it might be to curry favour with the lowest class, should keep a stiff attitude on the question of collectivism and property. The whole financial system of the Revolution, endorsed by the

Convention as by its predecessors, was based on the private proprietorship of land and on increasing the number of small proprietors. Not only was the Convention bound to maintain the effect of the large sales of national lands that had already taken place, but the prejudices and temper of its members made in the same direction. Robespierre, trying to reconcile the narrow logic of a lawyer with the need of pleasing his ardent supporters, based his position on a charitable and not on a political motive: "Public assistance is a sacred debt of Society. Society is under the obligation of securing a living for all its members, either by procuring work for them, or by securing the necessaries of existence to those who are past work."

Although the Convention maintained a conservative attitude in regard to the question of real property, it was decidedly inclined towards a confiscatory policy in all that related to personal wealth. This did not, however, become well marked until after the conclusion of the great struggle between the Mountain and the Gironde, which entered its last phase in May.

On the 12th of that month the Convention voted the formation of an army of *sans-culottes* for the defence of Paris, a measure of more significance for the internal than for the external affairs of France. On the 14th the Gironde made their reply by reading an address of the city of Bordeaux offering to march to Paris to help the Convention. On the 15th the Commune proceeded to appoint one of its nominees as provisional-general of the national guard of Paris. And on the following day the Girondins, alarmed into an attempt at action, proposed to the assembly that the municipal authorities of Paris should be removed from office and that the substitutes for the deputies to the Convention should be assembled at Bourges in case the Convention itself should be attacked and destroyed. This last proposal was highly characteristic of the Girondins, heroic as orators, but as members of a political party always timid of action.

The Committee of Public Safety, already tuned to its higher duties and viewing the faction fight of the assembly with some slight degree of detachment, steered a middle and politic course. Barère proposed a compromise, which the Girondins weakly accepted. But its enemies continued strenuous action, formed a new insurrectional committee, and set Hébert's infamous sheet, the *Père Duchesne*, howling for their blood. This newspaper deserves a few lines.

Hébert, a man of the middle class, after a stormy youth drifted into revolutionary journalism. With much verve, and a true Voltairian spirit, he at first took up a moderate attitude, but being a time server soon discovered that his interest lay in another direction. From the middle of 1792 he rose rapidly to great popularity by his loud defence of extreme courses. The *Père Duchesne,* copies of which are at this day among the greatest of bibliographical curiosities, was written for the people and in a jargon out-Heroding their own, a compound of oaths and obscenities. The *Père Duchesne* was nearly always in a state of *grande joie* or of *grande colère,* and at the epoch we have reached his anger is being continuously poured out, the filthiest stream of invective conceivable, against the Girondins.

With Marat and Hébert fanning the flames, the insurrectional committee drew up a new list of 32 suspect deputies. The Committee of Public Safety, appealed to by the Girondins, ordered the arrest of Hébert. On the following day, the 25th of May, the Commune demanded his release. Isnard, one of the Gironde, that day acting as president of the Convention, answered the deputation of the Commune with unbridled anger, and concluded by declaring that if Paris dared to lay one finger on a member of the Convention, the city would be destroyed. There was in this an unfortunate echo of the Duke of Brunswick's manifesto.

On the 26th Robespierre, at the Jacobin Club, gave his formal assent to the proposal that an insurrection should be organized against the Gironde. Two days later Hébert was released, and the Commune and the committees of the sections began organizing the movement. As a first step Hanriot, a sottish but very determined battalion leader, was placed in supreme command of the national guard.

The movement took place on the 31st of May. On that day the Convention was subjected to the organized pressure of a mob of about 30,000 men, the greater part national guards. The Convention was not invaded, however, nor was there any attempt, any desire, to suppress it as an institution. For the leaders fully realized that it was by maintaining the Convention as a figurehead that they could continue the fiction that the Government of France was not local, or Parisian, but national, or French. But while refraining from a direct attack on the Convention they subjected it to a pressure so strong and so long continued that they converted it, as they intended, into an organ of their will.

For three days Hanriot and his men remained at the doors of the Convention, and for three days, with growing agitation, the members within wrestled with the problem thus insistently presented at the point of bayonets and at the mouth of cannon. Motions of all sorts, some logical, some contradictory, were presented. Robespierre moved the arrest of twenty of his colleagues. The Committee of Public Safety, anxious to retain supreme power, tried for some middle course that might satisfy the mob. Barère proposed that, to relieve the Convention from its difficulty, the Girondins should pronounce their own exclusion from the assembly. The impetuous Isnard, one of the few attacked members present, accepted. This was on the 2d of June.

On the basis of the self-exclusion of the Girondin deputies the Committee of Public Safety now believed it could regain control of the situation, thereby demonstrating that it had formed an inadequate estimate of Hanriot. It decided to proclaim the suppression of the insurrectional committee, and it announced this to Hanriot at the same time as the self-exclusion of the Girondins. But Hanriot, sitting his horse at the doors of the Convention, was resolute and tipsy, a man of the sword not to be moved by parliamentary eloquence. He declined to accept any compromise, and ordered his guns to be brought up and unlimbered. The Convention was immediately stampeded by this act of drunken courage. The members attempted to escape. But every avenue, every street was closed by Hanriot's national guard, and Marat, blandly triumphant, led the members back to the hall sacred to their deliberations. There, ashamed and exhausted, at eleven o'clock that night, the Convention mutilated itself, suspended twenty-two of its members, and ordered the arrest of twenty-nine others.

CHAPTER XIII

THE REIGN OF TERROR

FOR six weeks after the fall of the Gironde, until the 13th of July, the course of events in France, both in Paris and in the provinces, reflected the bitterness of the two factions, conqueror and conquered. In a minor way, it also revealed the fundamental difference of attitude between the two wings of the successful party, between Danton, content to push the Girondins out of the way of the national policy, and Robespierre, rankling to destroy those who offended his puritanical and exclusive doctrine.

The Girondins had behind them a strong country backing; they had always been the advocates of the provinces against Paris; some of them had declared for federalism, for local republics, semi-independent states centring about Lyons, Marseilles, Bordeaux. Those who succeeded in escaping from Paris, made their way to where they might obtain support, and found, here and there, arms open to receive them. Lyons had risen against the Government on the 29th of May, and had rid itself of the Jacobin committee headed by Chalier, that had so far held it under control. Marseilles followed the example of Lyons. Normandy, where a considerable group of the fugitive deputies sought refuge, began to make preparations for marching on the capital.

This was serious enough. But two other dangers, each greater, threatened Paris. The military situation on the northern frontier was still no better, while the Vendéens were advancing from success to success, were increasing the size, the confidence, the efficiency of their armies. In such a desperate situation Danton seemed the only possible saviour, and for a few weeks he had his way. New generals were appointed; Custine to the Netherlands, Beauharnais to the Rhine, Biron to the Vendée; and at the same time negotiations were opened with the powers. But fortune refused to smile on Danton. Ill success met him at every turn, and opened the way to power for Robespierre. On the 10th of June the Vendéens captured the town of Saumur on the Loire, giving them a good passage for carrying operations to the northern side of the river. A council of war decided that an advance should be made into Brittany and Normandy, both strongly disaffected to the Convention. In the latter province Brissot and Buzot were already actively forming troops for the projected march against Paris. But before advancing to the north the Vendéen generals decided that it was imperative they should capture the city of Nantes, which controls all the country about the mouth of the Loire. Preparations were made accordingly, and, as the Vendéens had no siege train, Cathelineau and Charette headed a desperate assault against the city on the 29th of June. Cathelineau was killed. Nantes defended itself bravely. The Vendéens were thrown back, and, as many writers have thought, their failure at that point and at that moment saved the Republic

Apart from this one success, everything had been going ill with Danton's measures, and the Robespierrists were making corresponding headway. On the 10th of July the Committee of Public Safety was reconstituted, and Danton was not re-elected. Couthon and St. Just joined it, and Robespierre himself went on two weeks later; among the other members Barère for the moment followed Robespierre, while Carnot accepted every internal measure, concentrating all his energy on the administration of the war department.

It was just at this instant, with the Vendéens for the moment checked, that Normandy made its effort. On the 13th of July its army under the Baron de Wimpffen, a constitutional monarchist, was met by a Parisian army at Pacy, 30 miles from the capital. The Normans met with defeat, a defeat they were never able to retrieve.

On the same day a dramatic event was occurring at Paris,—the last despairing stroke of the Gironde against its detested opponents. From Caen, where Brissot and Buzot had been helping to organize Wimpffen's army, there had started for the capital a few days previously a young woman, Charlotte Corday. Full of enthusiasm, like Madame Roland, for the humanitarian ideals that blended so largely with the passions of the Revolution, she represented in its noblest, most fervent form that French provincial liberalism that looked to the Girondins for leadership. Like them she detested the three great figures who had led the Parisian democracy through massacre to its triumph,—Danton, Robespierre, Marat. And of the three it was Marat who worked deepest on her imagination, Marat always baying for blood, always scenting fresh victims, always corrupting opinion with his scum of printer's ink and poison. To Charlotte Corday it appeared that in this one individual all that was noble and beautiful in the Revolution was converted into all that was hideous and ignoble; and she slowly began to perceive that even a feeble woman like herself could remove that blot from France, if only she could find the courage. . .

On the 13th of July, Charlotte Corday, accomplished her twofold sacrifice. She gained admission to Marat's house and stabbed him in his bath; she meekly but courageously accepted the consequences. After being nearly lynched by the mob, she was tried by the Revolutionary Tribunal, and sent to the guillotine.

The Prussians captured Mainz on the 23rd of July, the Austrians Valenciennes on the 28th. These disasters enabled Robespierre and the Commune to impose their views as to the conduct of the military affairs of the Republic. Decrees were passed for purifying the army. The aristocrat generals, Beauharnais, Biron, Custine, were removed, and, eventually, were all sent to the scaffold. *Sans-culottes,* some honest, some capable, many dishonest, many incapable, replaced them. Sans-culottism reigned supreme. Civic purity became the universal test; and on this shibboleth the Commune inaugurated a system of politics of which the Tammany organization in New York offers the most conspicuous example at the beginning of the 20th century. Hébert was the party boss; his nominees filled the offices; graft was placed on the order of the day. The ministry of war and its numerous contracts became the happy hunting ground of the Parisian politician,—Hébert himself, on one occasion, working off an edition of 600,000 copies of his *Père Duchesne* through that ministry. And lastly one must add that the army of the interior, the army facing the Vendée fell into the hands of the politicians. An incapable drunkard, Rossignol, was placed in command instead of Biron who, after two victories over the Vendéens, was dismissed, imprisoned and sent to the guillotine.

It was perhaps necessary that a brave and dashing soldier of the old school like Biron should be removed from command, if the decrees of the Convention for prosecuting the war against the Vendée were to be carried out. One of those decrees ordered that "the forests shall be razed, the crops cut down, the cattle seized. The Minister of War shall send combustible materials of all sorts to burn the woods, brush, and heath." That was the spirit now entering the Revolution, the fury of destruction, the dementia of suspicion, the reign of terror.

The terrorists were of two sorts, the men of faction like Hébert, together with those who accepted terrorism reluctantly but daringly like Danton; with them terror was a political weapon. With Robespierre, however, and his Jacobin stalwarts, it was something more, a strangely compounded thing, a political weapon in a sense, but a weapon behind which stood a bigot, a fanatic, a temperament governed by jealous fears and by the morbid revengefulness of the man of feeble physique. It was Robespierre who always stood for the worst side of terrorism, for all that was most insidious and deep seated in it; and after its failure and the reaction in the summer of 1794, it was his name that was deservedly associated with the reign of terror.

Robespierre in the summer of 1793 was still logically maintaining his attitude; while Danton fought the enemies of the Republic, he fought Danton's measures. He told the Jacobin Club that it was always the same proposal they had to face, new levies, new battalions, to feed the great butchery. The plan of the enemies of the people,—he did not yet dare declare that Danton was one of them,—was to destroy the republic by civil and foreign war. In a manuscript note found after his death, he says "The interior danger comes from the bourgeois; to conquer them one must rally the people. The Convention must use the people and must spread insurrection. . . ." In August, carrying his thought a step further, he appeals to the Jacobin Club against the traitors whom he sees in everyone whose opinion diverges a hair's breadth from his own. There are traitors, he declares, even on the Committee of Public Safety, and all traitors must go to the guillotine.

At the moment this speech was delivered Admiral Lord Hood had just captured Toulon, while Marseilles was being attacked by Carteaux at the head of an army acting for the Convention. Coburg, commanding the Austrian forces in the Netherlands, was gaining a series of minor successes, and his cavalry was not much more than four days' march from Paris. Provisions were being gathered into the city by requisition, that is, by armed columns operating in the neighbouring departments. Confiscatory measures passed the Convention for raising a forced loan of 1,000,000,000 francs, for converting "superfluous" income to the use of the State,—a policy of poor man against rich.

Alongside of these measures terrorism was getting into full swing. The revolutionary tribunal had its staff quadrupled on the 5th of September; within a few days the sections were given increased police powers; and Collot d'Herbois and Billaud-Varennes, the two strongest supporters of Hébert in the Convention were elected to the Committee of Public Safety. On the 17th was passed the famous *Loi des suspects,* the most drastic, if not the first, decree on that burning question. It provided that all partisans of federalism and tyranny, all enemies of liberty, all *ci-devant* nobles not known for their attachment to the new institutions, must be arrested; and further that the section committees must draw up lists of suspects residing within their districts. All this meant a repetition on a larger and better organized plan of the massacres of a year before. As Danton had said in the debates on the Revolutionary Tribunal: "This tribunal will take the place of that supreme tribunal, the vengeance of the people; let us be terrible so as to dispense the people from being terrible." Judicial, organized terror was to replace popular, chaotic terror.

With terror now organized, the prisons filled, and the Revolutionary Tribunal sending victims to the guillotine daily, the internal struggle became one between two terrorist parties, of Hébert and of Robespierre, both committed to the policy of the day, but with certain differences. Hébert viewed the system as one affording personal safety,—the executioner being safer than the victim,—and the best opportunity for graft. The man of means was singled out by his satellites for suspicion and arrest, and was then informed that a judicious payment in the right quarter would secure release. Beyond that, Hébert probably cared little enough one way or the other; he was merely concerned in extracting all the material satisfaction he could out of life. With Robespierre the case was different; it was a struggle for a cause, for a creed, a creed of which he was the only infallible prophet. Poor, neat, respectable, unswerving but jealous, he commanded wide admiration as the type of the incorruptible democrat; stiffly and self-consciously he was reproducing the popular pose of Benjamin Franklin. Between him and Hébert there could be no real union. He was willing, while Hébert remained strong in his hold on the public, to act alongside of him, but that was all.

Under the pressure of the Commune and the Mountain, the Convention put the laws of terror in force against the defeated Gironde on the 3rd of October. Forty-three deputies, including Philippe *Egalité,* were sent to the tribunal, and about one hundred others were outlawed or ordered under arrest. The Convention, having thus washed its hands before the public, now felt able to make a stand against the increasing encroachments of the Commune, and on the 10th St. Just proposed that the Government should continue revolutionary till the peace, which meant that the Committee of Public Safety should govern and the constitution remain suspended.

The Committee showed as much vigour in dealing with the provinces as it showed feebleness in dealing with Paris. Through August and September, rebellious Lyons had been besieged; early in October it fell. The Committee proposed a decree which the Convention accepted,—from June 1793 to July 1794 it accepted everything,—declaring that Lyons should be razed to the earth. Couthon was sent to carry out this draconian edict, but proved too mild. At the end of October Collot d'Herbois, Fouché and 3,000 Parisian *sans-culottes* were sent down, and for awhile all went well. Houses were demolished, and executions were got in hand with so much energy that cannon and grape shot had to be used to keep pace with the rapidity of the sentences. About three thousand persons in all probably perished.

It was at this moment that in Paris the guillotine, working more slowly but more steadily than Fouché's cannon and grape, was claiming some of its most illustrious victims. From the 12th to the 15th of October, the Revolutionary Tribunal had to deal with the case of Marie Antoinette. The Queen, who had been treated with increased severity since the execution of the King, supported the attacks of the pitiless public prosecutor, Fouquier-Tinville, with firmness and dignity. The accusations against her were of the same general character as those against Louis, and require no special comment. But an incident of the trial brought out some of the most nauseous aspects of the Hébert régime. The Commune had introduced men of the lowest type at the Temple, had placed the Dauphin in the keeping of the infamous cobbler Simon, had attempted to manufacture filthy evidence against the Queen. Hébert went into the witness box to sling mud at her in person, and it was at that moment only, with a look and a word of reply that no instinct could mistake, that she forced a murmur of indignation or sympathy from the public. Robespierre was dining when he heard of the incident, and in his anger with Hébert broke his plate over the table.

The Queen went to the guillotine, driven in an open cart, on the 16th. A week later the Girondins went to trial, twenty-one deputies, among them Brissot, Vergniaud, Gensonné and Boyer Fonfrède. Their trial lasted five days, and among its auditors was Camille Desmoulins,—Desmoulins, whose pamphlets had helped place his unfortunate opponents where they stood, Desmoulins, whose heart, whose generosity was stirred, who already was revolting against terrorism, who was suddenly overwhelmed with a wave of remorse when sentence of death was pronounced against the men of the Gironde. It was the first revolt of opinion against the reign of terror, the first perceptible movement of the conscience of France, and it was to send Desmoulins himself to the guillotine.

The Girondins went to the scaffold on the 31st of October. The Duc d'Orléans on the 6th of November; four days later Madame Roland, who met death perhaps a little pedantically but quite nobly; then, on the 12th, Bailly. Of the Girondins who had escaped from Paris several committed suicide, Roland on receiving news of his wife's death; others within the next few months, Condorcet, Pétion, Buzot.

In this same month of November 1793 was introduced the Revolutionary Calendar, of which more will be said in the last chapter.[1] The holy seventh day disappeared in favour of the anti-clerical tenth day, Décadi; Saints' days and Church festivals were wiped out. This new departure was a step forward in the religious question which, a few weeks later, brought about an acute crisis.

Between October and December the climax and the turn were reached in the Vendean war. After heavy fighting in October Henri de La Rochejacquelein had invaded Brittany, defeating the Republicans at Chateau Gontier

[1] See Chap. XVII.

on the 25th. Rossignol now had under his orders the garrison of Mainz and two excellent subordinates in Kléber and Marceau, who succeeded, in spite of their commander, in wresting success at last. On the 13th of December a tremendous struggle took place at Le Mans in which the Vendéens were beaten after a loss of about 15,000 men. Kléber gave them no respite but a few days later cut up the remnants at Savenay. Although fighting continued long afterwards this proved the end of the Vendean grand army.

These victories were immediately followed by judicial repression. The *conventionnel* Carrier organized a Revolutionary Tribunal at Nantes, and committed worse horrors than Fouché had at Lyons. Finding a rate of 200 executions a day insufficient he invented the *noyade*. River barges were taken, their bottoms were hinged so as to open conveniently, and prisoners, tied in pairs, naked and regardless of sex, were taken out in them, and released into the water. At Nantes, like at Arras and several other points, the proceedings of the Revolutionary Tribunals and of the gangs who worked the prisons, were marked by gross immorality in dealing with the women prisoners. At Nantes, Carrier, most thorough and most infamous of the Terrorists, is said to have caused the death of 15,000 persons in four months.

The fury of the Revolution, which turned to frenzy and dementia at Nantes, blazed into a marvellous flame of patriotic energy on the frontiers. Nearly half a million men were enrolled in the course of 1793. A new volunteer battalion was added to each battalion of the old army, the new unit being named a *demi-brigade*. Rankers were pushed up to high command, partly by political influence, partly for merit. Jourdan, an old soldier, a shopkeeper, became general of the army of the north, and on the 15th of October defeated Coburg at Wattignies. The brilliant Hoche, ex-corporal of the French guards, was placed at the head of the army of the Moselle. Pichegru, the son of a peasant, took over the army of the Rhine. Under these citizen generals new tactics replaced the old. Pipeclay and method gave way to Sans-culottism and dash. The greatest of the generals of the Revolution said: "I had sooner see a soldier without his breeches than without his bayonet." Rapidity, surprise, the charging column, the helter-skelter pursuit, were the innovations of the new French generals. They translated into terms of tactics and strategy, Danton's famous apostrophe, "Audacity, more audacity, yet more audacity!"

CHAPTER XIV

THERMIDOR

DANTON had fallen fast in popularity and influence since the moment when, after the fall of the Gironde, he had appeared to dominate the situation. On the 12th of October, weary, sick at heart, disgusted at the triumph of the Hébertists, he had left Paris and, apparently retiring from politics, had gone back to his little country town of Arcis-sur-Aube. There a month later Robespierre sought him out, and invited him to joint action for pulling down Hébert. With Robespierre this meant no more than that Danton could help him, not that he would ever help Danton, and doubtless the latter realized it; but the bold course always drew him, and he accepted. Danton returned to Paris on the 21st of November.

Robespierre had been moved to this step by an alarming development of Hébertism. Anticlericalism, hatred of the priest,—and among other things the priest stood behind the Vendéen,—Voltairianism, materialism, all these elements had come to a head; and the clique who worked the Commune had determined that the triumph of the Revolution demanded the downfall of Catholicism, which was, as it seemed, equivalent to religion. A wave of atheism swept through Paris. To be atheistic became the mark of a good citizen. Gobel, the archbishop, and many priests, accepted it, and renounced the Church. Then a further step was taken. On the 10th of November the Cathedral of Notre Dame was dedicated to Reason, a handsome young woman from the opera personifying the goddess. Two weeks later, just as Danton reached Paris, the Commune closed all the churches of the city for the purpose of dedicating them to the cult of Reason.

Robespierre, like most of the men of the Revolution, was an enemy of the Church; but he was not an atheist. On the contrary he accepted in a very literal, dogmatic and zealous way the doctrines of Rousseau, his prophet not only in politics but in religion. To Robespierre the Hébertist cult of Reason was as gross blasphemy as it was to the most ardent Catholic, and the Jacobin leader had nerved himself for a struggle to destroy that cult. That was why he had appealed to Danton, though he knew that if Danton joined him in the fight it would not be for conscience, for a religious motive, but solely to destroy Hébert and perhaps to regain control of the Committee of Public Safety. This last possibility Robespierre risked.

The two allies immediately opened their campaign against Hébert. In the Convention Danton, with rather hollow rhetoric, declaimed in favour of popular festivals at which incense should be offered to the Supreme Being. Robespierre at the Jacobins, allowing his venom to master his logic, declared: "Atheism is aristocratic. The idea of a Supreme Being who guards injured innocence and who punishes triumphant crime is democratic. . . . If God did not exist we should have to invent Him."

It was just at this moment, when Hébertism and terrorism appeared interchangeable terms, and when the two most powerful men of the assembly had simultaneously turned against Hébertism, that Desmoulins stepped forward as the champion of the cause of mercy, to pull down Hébert, and with Hébert the guillotine. Early in December he brought out a newspaper once more, *Le Vieux Cordelier,* and in that boldly attacked the gang of thieves and murderers who were working the politics of the city of Paris. Public opinion awakened; voices were raised here and there; presently petitions began to flow in to the Convention. The tide was unloosened. How far would it go?

Robespierre, crafty, cunning, shifty, at first cautiously used Desmoulins for his purposes. But when Danton himself, the arch-terrorist, bravely accepted the doctrine of clemency, Robespierre began to draw back. At the end of December the return of Collot d'Herbois from his massacres at Lyons stiffened Robespierre, and rallied the Committee of Public Safety more firmly to the policy of terror. For some weeks a desperate campaign of words was fought out inch by inch, Danton and Desmoulins lashing out desperately as the net closed slowly in on them; and it was not till the 20th of February 1794 that they received the death stroke. It was dealt by St. Just.

St. Just, a doctrinaire and puritan nearly as fanatical as his chief, possessed what Robespierre lacked,—decision, boldness, and a keen political sense. On his return from a mission to the armies he had found in Paris the situation already described, and decided immediately to strike hard, at once, and at all the opponents of his party. The first measures were aimed at Hébert and the Commune, for St. Just judged that they were ripe for the guillotine. A decree was pushed through the Convention whereby it was ordered that the property of all individuals sent to the scaffold under the *Loi des suspects* should be distributed to the poor *sans-culottes*. This infamous enactment was intended to cut from under the feet of the Commune any popular support it still retained.

At St. Just's provocation the attacked party closed its ranks,—the Commune, the ministers, the Cordeliers, Hébert, Hanriot. Proclamations were issued for a new insurrection. But Paris was getting weary of insurrections, wearier still of the obvious blackguardism and peculation of the Hébertists, weariest of the perpetual drip of blood from the guillotine. No insurrection could be organized. For some days the opponents remained at arm's length. Finally on the 17th of March the Committee of Public Safety ordered the arrest of Hébert, Pache, Chaumette and a number of their prominent supporters, and was almost surprised to find that the arrest was carried out with virtually no opposition. Paris raised not a finger to defend them, and contentedly watched them go to the guillotine a week later.

It was otherwise with Danton. St. Just gave him no time. With the Committee and the Convention well in hand he struck at once, less than a week after Hébert had been despatched. He read a long accusation against Danton to the Convention, and that body weakly voted his arrest. Danton, Desmoulins, and some of their chief supporters were hurried to prison; and from prison to the Revolutionary Tribunal. On the 2d, 3rd and 4th of April they were tried by the packed bench and packed jury of that expeditious institution. But so uncertain was the temper of the vast throng that filled the streets outside, so violently did Danton struggle to burst his bonds, that for a moment it seemed as though the immense reverberations of his voice, heard, it is said, even across the Seine, might awaken the force of the people, as so often before, and overthrow the Jacobin rule. A hasty message to the Committee of Public Safety,—a hasty decree rushed through the Convention,—and Danton's voice was quelled, judgment delivered before the accused had finished his defence. On the next day Danton and Desmoulins went to the guillotine together,—Paris very hushed at the immensity and suddenness of the catastrophe. Desmoulins was gone, the leader of the revolt against the monarchy in 1789, the generous defender of the cause of mercy in 1794; and Danton was gone, with all his sins, with all his venality, the most powerful figure of the Revolution, more nearly the Revolution itself than any man of his time.

Complete triumph! As Robespierre, St. Just and Couthon looked about them, the three apostles leading France down the narrow path of civic virtue, they saw nothing but prostrate enemies. The power of the Commune was gone, and in its stead the Committee of Public Safety virtually ruled Paris. Danton, the possible dictator, the impure man ready to adjust compromises with the enemies of liberty, lax in conscience and in action, Danton too was down. The solid phalanx of the Jacobin Club, the remnant of the Commune, the Revolutionary Tribunal, stood solidly arrayed behind Robespierre; and the Convention voted with perfect regularity and unanimity every decree it was asked for.

But this attitude of the Convention only represented the momentary paralysis of fear. No one would venture on debate, leave alone opposition. Men like Sieyès attended punctiliously day after day, month after month, and never opened their lips,—only their eyes, watching the corner of the Mountain, whence the reeking oracle was delivered. In the city it was the same. The cafés, so tumultuous and excited at the opening of the Revolution, are oppressively silent now. A crowd gathers in the evening to hear the gazette read, but in that crowd few dare to venture a word, an opinion; occasional whispers are exchanged, the list of those sent to the guillotine is eagerly listened to, and then all disperse.

And the prisons are full,—of aristocrats, of suspects, of wealthy bourgeois. Those who have money occasionally buy themselves out, and generally succeed in living well; while outside the prison doors, angry, half-demented women revile the aristocrats who betray the people and who, even in prison, eat delicate food and drink expensive wines. Among the prisoners there is some light-heartedness, much demoralization, with here and there, at rare intervals, a Madame Roland or an André Chénier, to keep high above degradation their minds and their characters. And every day comes the heartrending hour of the roll call for the Revolutionary Tribunal which with so many means death.

The Tribunal itself, loses more and more

any sense of legality it had at the outset. Its procedure still carries a semblance of legal method, but it is really an automatic machine for affixing a legal label on political murders. And the Tribunal, as it progresses in its career, becomes more and more insane in its hatred of the party it seeks to destroy, of the anti-revolutionist, of the aristocrat. Is it not recorded that it ordered the arrest of a little girl of 13, Mlle. de Chabannes, suspect "because she had sucked the aristocratic milk of her mother." The Tribunal acquitted one person in every five; up to the fall of Danton it had sent about 1,000 persons to the guillotine; during the three months of Robespierre's domination it was to send another 1,600, increasing its activity by hysterical progression. When Thermidor was reached, about thirty individuals was the daily toll of the executioner.

Robespierre triumphant immediately revealed all his limitations; he was not a successful statesman; he was only a successful religionist. His first care, therefore, was to attend to the dogma of the French people. He proposed that Décadi should be converted into a new Sabbath; he caused the dregs of the Hébertists, including Gobel, to be indicted for atheism when their turn came for the Revolutionary Tribunal. Robespierre sending a renegade Archbishop of Paris to the scaffold for atheism marks how very far the Revolution had moved since the days of the States-General at Versailles.

On the 7th of May, a month after Danton's death, Robespierre delivered a long speech before the Convention, a speech that marks his apogee. It was a high-flown rhapsody on civic morality and purism. Voltaire and the Encyclopedists were bitterly attacked; Jean Jacques Rousseau was deified. The State should adopt his religious attitude, his universal church of nature. In that church, nature herself is the chief priest and there is no need of an infamous priesthood. Its ritual is virtue; its festivals the joy of a great people. Therefore let the Convention decree that the Cult of the Supreme Being be established, that the duty of every citizen is to practise virtue, to punish tyrants and traitors, to succour the unfortunate, to respect the weak, to defend the oppressed, to do good unto others. Let the Convention institute competitions for hymns and songs to adorn the new cult; and let the Committee of

Public Safety,—that harassed and overburdened committee,—adjudicate, and reward the successful hymnologists.

The Convention listened in silence, disgust, silent rebellion,—but bowed its head. The new cult appealed to very few. Here and there an intellectual Rousseauist accepted it, but the mass did what mankind in all countries and ages has done, refused to reason out what was a religious and therefore an emotional question. To the vast majority of Frenchmen there was only one choice, catholicism or non-catholicism, and the cult of the Supreme Being was just as much non-catholicism as that of Reason.

Robespierre, blind and satisfied, went on his way rejoicing. On the 8th of June, as President of the Convention, he took the chief part in a solemn inauguration of the new religion. There were statues, processions, bonfires, speeches, and Robespierre, beflowered, radiant in a new purple coat, pontificating over all. But beneath the surface all was not well. The Convention had not been led through the solemn farce without protest. Words of insult were hissed by more than one deputy as Robespierre passed within earshot, and the Jacobin leader realized fully that behind the docile votes and silent faces currents of rage and protest were stirring. For this, as for every ill, there was but one remedy, to sharpen the knife.

Two days later, on the 10th, new decrees were placed before the Convention for intensifying the operations of the Revolutionary Tribunal. New crimes were invented "spreading discouragement, perverting public opinion"; the prisoner's defence was practically taken away from him; and, most important, members of the Convention lost their inviolability. The Convention voted the decree, but terror had now pushed it to the wall and self-defence automatically sprang up. From that moment the Convention nerved itself to the inevitable struggle. Billaud, Collot and Barère, the *impures* of the Committee of Public Safety, looked despairingly on all sides of the Convention for help to rid themselves of the monster, whose tentacles they already felt beginning to twine about them.

Just at this critical moment a trivial incident arose that pierced Robespierre's armour in its weakest joint, and that crystallized the fear of the Convention into ridicule,—ridicule that proved the precursor of revolt. Catherine Théot, a female spiritualist, or medium, as we should call her at the present day, highly elated at the triumph of the Supreme Being over the unemotional Goddess of Reason, had made Robespierre the hero of her half-insane inspirations. She now announced to her credulous devotees that she was the mother of God, and that Robespierre was her son. It became the sensation of the day. Profiting by the temporary absence of St. Just with the army in the Netherlands, the Committee of Public Safety decided that Catherine Théot was a nuisance and a public danger, and must be arrested. Robespierre, intensely susceptible to ridicule, not knowing what to do, pettishly withdrew from the Convention, confined himself to his house and the Jacobin Club, and left the Committee to carry out its intention. Every member of the Convention realized that this was a distinct move against Robespierre.

St. Just was with Jourdan's army in the north, and for the moment all eyes were fixed on that point. The campaign of 1794 might be decisive. France and Austria had put great armies in the field. The latter now controlled the belt of frontier fortresses, and if, pushing beyond these, she destroyed the French army, Paris and the Revolution might soon be at an end. As the campaign opened, however, fortune took her place with the tricolour flag. Minor successes fell to Moreau, Souham, Macdonald, Vandamme. In June the campaign culminated. The armies met south of Brussels at Fleurus on the 25th of that month. For fifteen hours the battle raged, Kléber with the French right wing holding his ground, the centre and left slowly driven back. But at the close of the day the French, not to be denied, came again. Jourdan, with St. Just by his side, drove his troops to a last effort, regained the lost ground, and more. The Austrians gave way, turned to flight, and one of the great victories of the epoch had been won. In a few hours the glorious news had reached Paris, and in Paris it was interpreted as an evil portent for Robespierre.

For if there existed something that could possibly be described as a justification for terrorism, that something was national danger and national fear. Ever since the month of July 1789 there had been a perfect correspondence between military pressure on Paris and the consequent outbreak of violence. But this great victory, Fleurus, seemed to mark the complete triumph of the armies of the Republic; all danger had been swept away, so why should terror and the guillotine continue? As the captured Austrian standards were paraded in the Tuileries gardens and presented to the Convention on a lovely June afternoon, every inclination, every instinct was for rejoicing and good will. The thought that the cart was still steadily, lugubriously, wending its way to the insatiable guillotine, appeared unbearable.

From this moment the fever of conspiracy against Robespierre coursed rapidly through the Convention. Some, like Sieyès, were statesmen, and judged that the turn of the tide had come. Others, like Tallien or Joseph Chénier, were touched in their family,—a brother, a wife, a sister, awaiting judgment and the guillotine. Others feared; others hoped; and yet others had vengeance to satisfy, especially the remnants of Danton's, of Brissot's and of Hébert's party. St. Just saw the danger of the situation and attempted to cow opposition. He spoke threateningly of the necessity for a dictatorship and for a long list of proscriptions.

It was the most silent member of the Committee of Public Safety, Carnot, who brought on the crisis. Affecting an exclusive concern for the conduct of the war and perfunctorily signing all that related to internal affairs, he was secretly restive and anxious to escape from the horrible situation. Prompted by some of his colleagues, he ordered, on the 24th of July, that the Paris national guard artillery should go to the front. This was taking the decisive arm out of the hands of Hanriot, for Hanriot had made his peace with Robespierre, had survived the fall of Hébert, and was still in command of the national guard.

There could be no mistaking the significance of Carnot's step. On the same night Couthon loudly denounced it at the Jacobins, and the club decided that it would petition the Convention to take action against Robespierre's enemies. Next day Barère replied. He read a long speech to the Convention in which, without venturing names, he blamed citizens who were not heartened by the victories of the army and who meditated further proscriptions. On the 26th, the 8th of Thermidor, Robespierre reappeared in the assembly, and ascended the tribune to reply to Barère.

Robespierre felt that the tide was flowing against him; instinct, premonitions, warned him that perhaps his end was not far off. In this speech—it was to be his last before the Convention—the melancholy note prevailed.

There was no effort to conciliate, no attempt at being politic, only a slightly disheartened tone backed by the iteration which France already knew so well:—the remedy for the evil must be sought in purification; the Convention, the Committee of Public Safety, must be purged.

Under the accustomed spell the Convention listened to the end. The usual motions were put. Robespierre left the assembly. It was voted that his speech should be printed; and that it should be posted in all the communes of France. For a moment it looked as though the iron yoke were immovably fixed. Then Cambon went to the tribune, and ventured to discuss Robespierre's views. Billaud followed. And presently the Convention, hardly realizing what it had done, rescinded the second of its two votes. Robespierre's speech should be printed, but it should not be placarded on the walls.

At the Jacobin Club the rescinded vote of the Convention conveyed a meaning not to be mistaken. Robespierre repeated his Convention speech, which was greeted with acclamations. Billaud and Collot were received with hoots and groans, were driven out, and were erased from the list of members. Through the night the Jacobins were beating up their supporters, threatening insurrection; and on their side the leaders of the revolt attempted to rally the members of the Convention to stand firmly by them.

The next day was the 9th of Thermidor. St. Just made a bold attempt to control the situation. Early in the morning he met his colleagues of the Committee of Public Safety and, making advances to them, promised to lay before them a scheme that would reconcile all the divergent interests of the Convention. While the Committee awaited his arrival he proceeded to the body of the Convention, obtained the tribune, and began a speech. Realizing how far the temper of the assembly was against him, he boldly opened by denouncing the personal ambitions of Robespierre, and by advocating moderate courses—but he had not gone far when the members of the Committee, discovering the truth, returned to the Convention, and set to work with the help of the revolted members, to disconcert him. St. Just had perhaps only one weakness, but it was fatal to him on the 9th of Thermidor, for it was a weakness of voice. He was silenced by interruptions that constantly grew stormier. Billaud followed him and made an impassioned attack on the Jacobins. Robespierre attempted to reply. But Collot d' Herbois was presiding, and Collot declined to give Robespierre the tribune. The din arose; shouts of "Down with the tyrant, down with the dictator," were raised. Tallien demanded a decree of accusation. Members pressed around the Jacobin leader, who at this last extremity tried to force his way to the tribune. But the way was barred; he could only clutch the railings, and, asking for death, looking in despair at the public galleries that had so long shouted their Jacobin approval to him, he kept crying: "La mort! la mort!" He had fallen. The whole Convention was roaring when Collot from the presidential chair announced the vote whereby Robespierre, St. Just. Couthon, Hanriot, and several others, were ordered under arrest.

Hanriot at this crisis again displayed his qualities of action. While the members of the Convention were wasting time in talk and self-congratulation, he was getting his forces together. He succeeded in freeing the accused deputies from their place of temporary arrest, and by the evening, all were gathered together at the Hotel de Ville. The Jacobins declared for Robespierre. The party made determined efforts through the evening to raise insurrection. But only small bodies of national guards could be kept together at the Hotel de Ville, and these began to dwindle away rapidly late in the evening when heavy rain fell.

Meanwhile the Convention had met again in evening session. It appointed one of its own members, Barras, to command all the military forces that could be mustered, and then voted the escaped deputies outlaws for having broken arrest. The western districts of the city rallied to the Convention. Barras showed energy and courage. Information reached him of the state of affairs at the Hotel de Ville, and at one o'clock in the morning of the 29th he rallied several sectional battalions and marched quickly against the Robespierrists.

At the Hotel de Ville there was little resistance. It was raining hard, and few remained with the Jacobin leaders. There was a short scuffle, in which Robespierre apparently attempted to kill himself and lodged a bullet in his jaw. The arrests were carried out, and a few hours later, no trial being necessary for outlaws, Robespierre, St. Just, Hanriot, Couthon and about twenty more, were driven through the streets to the guillotine.

CHAPTER XV

THE LAST DAYS OF THE CONVENTION

IT is hard when considering the extraordinary features of the reign of terror, to realize that in some directions it was accomplishing a useful purpose. If the Revolution had been maintained so long, in the face of anarchy, of reaction and of foreign pressure, it was only by a policy of devouring flames and demented angels. And meanwhile, whatever might be the value or the fate of republican institutions, unconsciously the great social revolution had become an accomplished fact. In the short space of five years,—but such years,—social equality, freedom of opportunity, a new national attitude, a new national life, had become ineradicable custom; the assemblies, in their calmer moments, had passed laws for educating and humanizing the French people, and every six months snatched from time and from Bourbon reaction for this purpose was worth some sort of price. When France rubbed her eyes after Thermidor, drew breath, and began to consider her situation, she found herself a vastly different France from that of 1789.

The whole course of the Revolution was like that of a rocket, rushing and whirring upwards, hesitating a moment, then bursting and scattering its fragments in a downward course to earth. Thermidor was the bursting point of the Revolution, and after Thermidor we enter into a descending period, when the shattered fragments gradually lose their flame, when the great inspiration of the Revolution dies out, and only the less grand, less terrible, less noble, less horrifying things remain. The track of those shattered fragments must now be followed.

The public interpreted the fall of Robespierre more accurately than did the Convention, and saw in it the end of the reign of terror rather than the end of an individual dictatorship. The nightmare was over; men began to breathe, to talk. From day to day, almost from hour to hour, the tide rose; rejoicing quickly showed signs of turning into reaction. Within two weeks of the fall of Robespierre it became necessary for the men who had pulled him down to affirm solemnly that the revolutionary government still existed, and would continue to exist. This the Convention declared by a formal vote on the 12th of August.

At the same time the Convention was returning to life, its members to self-assertion; and if its measures were chiefly directed to preventing for the future any such preponderance as Robespierre had exercised, they also rapidly tended to get in line with the opinion now loudly proclaimed in all directions against terrorism. Within a few weeks the Committee of Public Safety was increased in numbers and changed in personnel—among its new members, Cambecérès, Sieyès, Rewbell. Other committees took over enlarged powers. The Commune was suppressed, Paris being ruled by officials chosen by the Convention. But the sections were allowed to remain, for it was their support had given Barras victory on the 9th of Thermidor, and no one foresaw as yet that it was from the sections that the next serious danger would come.

The national guards, by a series of measures, were purged, and converted into an exclusively middle class organization. The Revolutionary Tribunal, after disposing of several large batches from the Robespierrists and the Commune, was reorganized though not suppressed. Its worst judges and officials were removed, its procedure was strictly legalized, and its activity was greatly moderated; it continued in existence, however, for about a year, and almost for lack of business came to an end in the spring of 1795.

The terrorists, who had really led the revolt against Robespierre, by gradual stages sank back. At the end of August, Collot, Billaud and Barère went off the Committee of Public Safety. Two weeks later Carrier's conduct at Nantes incidentally came before the Revolutionary Tribunal and a storm arose about him that finally destroyed any power the terrorists still retained. The press was seething with recovered freedom, and the horrors of Carrier gave the journalists a tremendous text. A long struggle was waged over him. In the Convention, Billaud and Collot, feeling that the attack on Carrier was in reality an attack against them and every other terrorist, tried hard to save him. It was not till December that the Convention finally decided to hand him over to justice and not till the 16th of that month that the Revolutionary Tribunal sent him to the guillotine.

Among the striking changes brought about by the reaction after Thermidor was that it put two extreme parties in violent antagonism, with the Convention and reasonable public opinion as a great neutral ground between them. One of these was the party of the defeated Jacobins, raging at their downfall, convinced that without their guidance the Republic must perish. The other was that of the *Muscadins,* the scented and pampered golden youth, led by the *conventionnel* Fréron, asserting loudly their detestation of sans-culottism and democratic raggedness, breaking heads with their sticks when opportunity offered. During the excitement of Carrier's trial the Muscadins made such violent demonstrations against the Jacobins that the Committee of Public Safety ordered the closing of the club. But neither the Committee nor the Muscadins could destroy the Jacobin himself.

Fleurus had been followed by continued success. Jourdan and Pichegru drove the Austrians before them and overran the Low Countries to the Rhine. Then in October Pichegru opened a winter campaign, invaded Holland, and, pushing on through snow and ice, occupied Amsterdam in January and captured the Dutch fleet, caught in the ice, with his cavalry under Moreau. At the same time Jourdan was operating further east, and, sweeping up the valley of the Rhine, cleared the Austrians from Köln and Coblenz. Further along the Rhine the Prussians now only held Mainz on the French side of that river. To the south the generals of the Republic occupied all the passes of the Alps into Italy, and pushed triumphantly into Spain. With their hand full of these successes the Committee of Public Safety opened peace negotiations at the turn of the year. With peace established the Committee would be able to transmit its power to a regular constitutional government.

As the year 1795 opened, the interior situation began to get acutely troublesome once more. Although the Convention was pursuing a temperate course, relaxing the rigour of the revolutionary legislation on all sides, its concessions did not satisfy, but only encouraged, the reactionary party. Worse than this, however, the winter turned out the worst since 1788, for shortage of food. The Parisian mob, however much it had now lost of its insurrectional vigour, felt starvation no less keenly than before, and hunger made doubly dangerous the continued strugglings of Jacobins and Muscadins for power. The Convention tried hard to steer a safe course between them.

Towards the middle of February it was the

Jacobins who appeared the more dangerous. In their irritation and fear of the collapse of the Republic they organized revolt. At Toulon, at Marseilles, they seized control, and were suppressed not without difficulty. The Convention thereupon ordered that the conduct of Billaud, Barère and Collot should be investigated. A few days later it recalled the members of the Gironde who had succeeded in escaping from the operations of the Revolutionary Tribunal, among them Louvet, Isnard, Lanjuinais. Alarmed at these steps, supported by the clamours of the starving for bread, the Paris Jacobins rose against the Convention. On the 1st of April,—the 12th of Germinal,—the assembly was invaded, and for four hours was in the hands of a mob shouting for bread and the Constitution. Then the national guard rallied, and restored order, and the Convention immediately decreed that Billaud, Barère and Collot should be deported to the colony of Guiana,—Guiana, the mitigated guillotine for nearly a century the vogue in French politics, the *guillotine sèche*. Barère's sinister saying: "Only the dead never come back," was not justified in his case. He alone of the three succeeded in evading the decreed punishment and lived, always plausible and always finding supporters, to the days of Louis Philippe, when he died obscurely.

This was a great success for the moderates. But to observers of the Revolution from a distance, from London, Berlin or Vienna, the event appeared under a slightly different light. Pichegru happened to be in Paris at the moment, and Pichegru had been made military commander of the city. In reality he had little to do with suppressing the insurrection, but from a distance it appeared that the Republic had found in its democratic general, the conqueror of Holland, that solid support of force without which the establishment of law and order in France appeared impossible.

A few days later the pacification began. At Basle Barthélemy had been negotiating for months past, and now, on the 5th of April, he signed a treaty with Hardenberg, the representative of Prussia. The government of King Frederick William was far too much interested in the third partition of Poland, then proceeding, far too little interested in the Rhineland, to maintain the war longer. It agreed to give the French Republic a free hand to the south of the Rhine in return for which it was to retain a free hand in northern Germany, an arrangement which was to underlie many important phases of Franco-Prussian relations from that day until 1871.

The peace with Prussia was followed by one with Holland on the 16th of March, which placed the smaller state under conditions approaching vassalage to France. But with England and Austria, closely allied, the war still continued, and that not only because Austria was as yet unwilling to face so great a territorial loss as that of the Netherlands, but also because the Committee of Public Safety was not yet anxious for a complete pacification. Already it was clear that the real force of the Republic lay in her armies, and the Convention did not desire the presence of those armies and their generals in Paris.

In the capital the situation continued bad from winter to spring, from spring to summer. As late as May famine was severe, and people were frequently found in the streets dead of starvation. To meet the general dissatisfaction Cambacérès brought in a proposal for a new constitution. But nothing could allay the agitation, and in May the reactionary party, now frankly royalist, caused serious riots in the south. At Marseilles, Aix and other towns many Jacobins were killed, and so grave did the situation appear that on the

10th the Committee of Public Safety was given enlarged powers, and throwing itself back, relaxed its severity against the Jacobins. Ten days later came a second famine riot, the insurrection of the 1st of Prairial, a mob honey-combed with Jacobin and reactionary agitators invading the Convention as in Germinal, and clamouring for bread and a constitution. The disorder in the assembly was grave and long continued. One member was killed. But the Government succeeded in getting national guards to the scene; and in the course of the next two days poured 20,000 regular troops into the city. Order was easily restored. Several executions took place. And the Convention voted the creation of a permanent guard for its protection.

Royalism had been raising its head fast since Thermidor. The blows of the Convention even after the 1st of Prairial, had been mostly aimed at Jacobinism. The royalists were looking to a new constitution as an opportunity for a moderate monarchical form of government, with the little Dauphin as king, under the tutelage of a strong regency that would maintain the essential things of the Revolution. Their aspirations were far from unreasonable, far from impossible, until, on the 10th of June, death barred the way by removing the young Prince. The details of his detention at the Temple are perhaps the most repellent in the whole history of the Revolution. Separated from his mother and his aunt, the Princess Elizabeth, who followed the Queen to the scaffold, he was deliberately ill used by Simon and those who followed him as custodians, so that after Thermidor he was found in an indescribable state of filth and ill health. His treatment after that date was improved, but his health was irretrievably broken, so that when, in the early part of 1795, the royalists and many moderates began to look towards the Temple for the solution of the constitutional question, the Committee of Public Safety began to hope for the boy's death. This hope was in part translated into action. The Dauphin was not given such quarters, such food, or such medical attendance, as his condition required, and his death was wilfully hastened by the Government. How important a factor he really was appeared by the elation displayed by the republicans over the event, for Louis XVII was a possible king, while Louis XVIII, for the moment, was not.

It was the Comte de Provence, brother of Louis XVI, who succeeded to the claim. He was one of the old Court; he had learned nothing in exile; he was associated with the detested *émigrés,* the men who had fought in Condé's battalions against the armies of the Republic. And as if all this were not enough to make public opinion hostile, he issued proclamations on the death of his nephew announcing his assumption of the title of King of France and his determination to restore the old order. Within a few days, a royalist expedition, conveyed on English ships, landed at Quiberon on the Breton coast, and fanned to fresh flame the embers of revolt still smouldering in Brittany and the Vendée.

Hoche had been placed in charge of Western France some months before this, and by judicious measures had fairly succeeded in pacifying the country. He met the new emergency with quick resource. Collecting a sufficient force, with great promptness he marched against the royalists, who had been joined by three or four thousand Breton peasants. He fought them back to Quiberon, cooped them up, stormed their position, gave no quarter, and drove a remnant of less than 2,000 back to their ships.

That was almost the end of the trouble in the west of France. There was still a little fighting in the Vendée, but after the capture and execution of Charette and Stofflet in the early part of 1796, Hoche was left master of the situation.

While the royalists were being shot down at Quiberon the Convention was debating a new constitution for France, a constitution no longer theoretical, no longer a political weapon with which to destroy the monarchy, but practical, constructive, framed by the light of vivid political experience, intended to maintain the Republic and to make of it an acceptable, working machine. What was decided on was this. The franchise which the Législative had extended to the working classes after the 10th of August, was to be withdrawn from them, and restricted once more to the middle class. There were to be two houses; the lower was to be known as the *Corps législatif,* or Council of Five Hundred; the upper was to be chosen by the lower, was to number only two hundred and fifty, and was to be known as the Ancients. The lower house was to initiate legislation; the upper one was to do little more than to exercise the suspensive veto which the Constitution of 1791 had given to the King. Then there was to be an executive body, and that was merely the Committee of Public Safety modified. There were to be five Directors elected for individual terms of five years, and holding general control over foreign affairs, the army and navy, high police and the ministries. The constitution further reaffirmed the declaration of the rights of man and guaranteed the sales of the national lands.

This constitution had many good points, was not ill adapted to the needs and aspirations of France in the year 1795, and it was hailed with delight by the public. This at first seemed a good symptom. But the Convention soon discovered that this delight was founded not so much on the excellence of the constitution, as on the fact that putting it into force would enable France to get rid of the Convention, of the men of the Revolution. This was a sobering thought.

After some consideration of this difficult point, the Convention decided, about the end of August, on a drastic step. To prevent the country from excluding the men of the Convention from the Council of Five Hundred, it enacted that two-thirds of the members of the new body must be taken from the old; this was the famous decree of the two-thirds, or decree of Fructidor. Now there was something to be said for this decree. It was, of course, largely prompted by the selfish motive of men who, having power, wished to retain it. But it could be urged that since the fall of Robespierre the Convention had steered a difficult course with some ability and moderation, and had evolved a reasonable constitution for France. Was it not therefore necessary to safeguard that constitution by preventing the electors from placing its execution in the hands of a totally untried body of men?

Whatever there might be to say in favour of the decrees of Fructidor, they provoked an explosion of disgust and disappointment on the part of the public. The sections of Paris protested loudly, sent petitions to the Convention asking for the withdrawal of the decrees, and, getting no satisfaction, took up a threatening attitude. The Convention had weathered worse-looking storms, however; it held on its course and appointed the 12th of October for the elections. The sections, led by the section Lepeletier, thereupon organized resistance.

On the 4th of October, 12th of Vendémiaire, the sections of Paris called out their national guard. The Convention replied by ordering General Menou, in command of the regular troops in the city, to restore order. Menou had few troops, and was weak. He failed; and that night the Convention suspended him, and, as in Thermidor, gave Barras supreme command. Barras acted promptly. He called to his help every regular army officer in Paris at that moment, among others a young Corsican brigadier, Buonaparte by name, and assigned troops and a post to each. He hastily despatched another young officer, Murat, with his hussars, to bring some field pieces into the city; and so passed the night.

On the next day the crisis came to a head. The national guards, between 20,000 and 30,000 strong, began their march on the Convention. They were firmly met at various points by the Government troops. General Buonaparte caught the insurgents in the rue St. Honoré at just a nice range for his guns, promptly poured grape in, and completely dispersed them.

Once more the Convention had put down insurrection, and once more it showed moderation in its victory. It only allowed two executions to take place, but held Paris down firmly with regular troops. Buonaparte, whom Barras already knew favourably, had made so strong an impression and had rendered such good service, that he was appointed second in command, and not long after got Barras' reversion and became general-in-chief of the army of the Interior.

With this last vigorous stroke the Convention closed its extraordinary career,—a career that began with the monarchy, passed through the reign of terror, and finished in the Directoire.

CHAPTER XVI

THE DIRECTOIRE

WITH the Directoire the Revolution enters its last phase, and with that phase all readers of history connect certain well-marked external characteristics, extravagance of dress, of manners, of living; venality and immorality unblushing and unrestrained. The period of the Directoire is that during which the political men of the Revolution, with no principles left to guide them, gradually rot away; while the men of the sword become more and more their support, and finally oust them from power.

The Councils, apart from the ex-members of the Convention, were found to be far less royalist than had been expected. The farming class, which had had great influence in the elections, had gained much from the Revolution; the farmers had got rid of the feudal burdens; they had acquired land; they had profited from free transit. Anxious to retain what they had won, they elected men of moderate views rather than reactionaries. The voice of these new members could not, however, influence the choice of the Directors, who were all taken from the ex-conventionnels. They were Barras, Rewbell, Carnot, Larevellière and Letourneur. Of these Letourneur and Carnot were ready to listen to the wishes of the electorate, and to join hands with the new party of moderates in a constructive policy. The other three however took their stand firmly on the maintenance of the settlement effected by the Convention, and on deriving all the personal advantage they could from power. Rewbell began to accumulate a vast fortune, and Barras to squander and luxuriate.

The officials appointed by the Directors were as needy and rapacious as their chiefs. Everything could be had for money. England and the United States were offered treaties on the basis of first purchasing the good will of ministers for Foreign Affairs or Directors. In the gilded halls of the Luxembourg, Barras, surrounded by a raffish court, dispensed the honours and the spoils of the new régime. Women in astounding and wilfully indecent dresses gravitated about him and his entourage, women representing all the strata heaved upwards by the Revolution, with here and there a surviving aristocrat, like the widow of Beauharnais, needy, and turning to the new sun to relieve her distress. Among them morality was at the lowest ebb. For the old sacrament of marriage had been virtually demolished by law; civil marriage and divorce had been introduced, and in the governing classes, so much affected in family life and fortune by the reign of terror, the step between civil marriage and what was no marriage at all soon appeared a distinction without much difference. There seemed only one practical rule for life, to find the means of subsistence, and to have as good a time as possible.

The external situation which the new Government had to face required energetic measures. There had been great hopes after the victories of 1794, that the year 1795 would see the French armies pressing into the valley of the Danube and bringing the Austrian monarchy to terms. But the campaign of 1795 went to pieces. The generals were nearly as venal as the politicians, and Pichegru was successfully tampered with. He failed to support Jourdan; he made false movements; and as a result the French armies at the close of the summer were no further than the Rhine.

Preparations were made by the Directoire to retrieve this comparative failure; the campaign of 1796 was to see a strong offensive against the Austrians to the north and to the south of the Alps. Jourdan and Moreau, the latter displacing Pichegru, were once more to attempt to penetrate towards Vienna by the valley of the Danube. At the same time a smaller army was to invade Italy and, from the valley of the Po, perhaps lend a helping hand to the armies in Germany. Buonaparte was selected for this last command.

Buonaparte owed his new appointment to a combination of reasons. He had for some time past, knowing the ground, placed plans for the invasion of Italy before the Government. These plans gave promise of success, and Carnot was ready to give their author a chance of carrying them into execution. Alongside of this was the strong personal impression made by Buonaparte; his capacity was unmistakable. And last of all came the element of romance,—he had fallen in love with Mme. de Beauharnais, protégée of Barras,—and Barras worked for the appointment. Early in March Napoleone Buonaparte and Joséphine de Beauharnais were married; before the end of the month the young general had reached his headquarters at Nice.

In the middle of April news reached Paris of a series of brilliant engagements in which the army of Italy had defeated the Austrians and Sardinians. But immediately afterwards the Directoire was faced by the unpleasant fact that their new general, disregarding his instructions, had concluded an armistice with Sardinia. Already in less than a month, Bonaparte, as he now called himself, had shown that he was a great general, and moreover a politician who might become a danger to the Directoire itself. From that moment a veiled struggle began between the two, the Directoire attempting to reduce the power and influence of its general, Bonaparte constantly appealing from the Directoire to the public by rhetorical accounts of his victories and proceedings.

While Bonaparte was invading Lombardy and attacking the great Austrian fortress of Mantua, the Directoire had to deal with conspiracy in Paris. Conspiracy was a striking feature of the period that followed the fall of Robespierre; in fact, for the ten years that follow it may be said that all internal politics revolve about conspiracies. One of the most noteworthy was the one that came to a head in the spring of 1796, under the lead of Babeuf.

Babeuf was a revolutionist of extreme views, but views rather social than political. His experience before the Revolution had been that of a surveyor and land agent, and in this business he had apparently gone below the surface and had thought over that great nexus of social, political, and economic questions that centre on that of the proprietorship of the soil. The Revolution turned him into a collectivist, and with the Directoire in power, and a middle class reaction in full swing, Babeuf began to be an influence. The Revolution had so far produced popular leaders, but not popular leaders who were of the people, and whose policy was for the people. Mirabeau and Danton looked to the people, but only as opportunist statesmen. Hébert had imitated the people, but for the sake of his own advancement. Robespierre, more honestly, had attempted to be the prophet of the people, but with him democracy was only the sickly residue of Rousseau's *Contrat Social,* and when it came to measures, to social legislation, he proved only a narrow bourgeois and lawyer. And so it had been all the way through; the people, the great national battering-ram that Danton had guided, remained a mass without expression. The people had never had leaders of their own, had never had a policy save for their demand for a vote and for the blood of their oppressors. And now here was a man of the people who had a popular policy, who put his finger on the question that lay even deeper than that of privilege, that of proprietorship.

Babeuf's doctrine was collectivist. Nature has given every man an equal right to enjoy her benefits; it is the business of society to maintain this equality; Nature imposes the obligation of labour, but both labour and enjoyment must be in common; monopolizing benefits of land or industry is a crime; there should be neither rich men nor poor; nor should there be individual proprietorship of land,—the earth is no man's property.

These doctrines were fervently accepted by a small group of devoted followers; they were widely acquiesced in by Jacobin malcontents seeking a convenient arm against the Government. Clubs were formed, the *Cercle des Egaux,* the *Club du Panthéon;* propaganda was carried on; conspiracy was evolved. Wholesale efforts were made to gain over the police and some troops. Finally the Directoire got wind of the proceedings, and by prompt measures broke up the conspiracy and captured its leaders. Babeuf, arrested on the 10th of May, was sentenced to death a year later by a special court, and executed.

On the 19th of May the Directoire endorsed Bonaparte's action by signing a favourable peace with Sardinia; then taking advantage of his further successes at Lonato and Castiglione, it half bullied, half bribed the feeble Government of Spain into a treaty of alliance offensive and defensive, the treaty of San Ildefonso, signed on the 19th of August. This placed a redoubtable naval force in line against England, with the immediate result that she withdrew her fleet from the Mediterranean where it had been considerably impeding the operations of the French generals along the Italian seaboard. Before the close of the year the Directoire pushed a step further, and Hoche made an attempt, frustrated by bad weather, to disembark in Ireland, which was ready to revolt against England. In February 1797, however, Admiral Jervis crushed the Spanish fleet off Cape St. Vincent, restoring by this stroke England's commanding position at sea.

In Germany matters had not gone well with

the Republic. The young Archduke Charles, massing cleverly against Jourdan, drove him back to the Rhine before Moreau could effect his junction. Moreau had nothing left but retreat. This success enabled the Austrian Government to reinforce its troops in the Tyrol, whence its generals made repeated efforts to drive Bonaparte from the siege of Mantua. In September he won a considerable victory over the Austrians at Bassano; in November at Arcola; in January at Rivoli. Finally in February Mantua surrendered; Bonaparte in less than twelve months had disposed of five Austrian armies and captured the stronghold of the Hapsburgs in Italy.

Preparations were now made for a new move. The Directoire withdrew Bernadotte with a strong division from Germany to strengthen Bonaparte, and raised his army to 70,000 men. He advanced through Friuli and the Julian Alps, outflanking the Archduke Charles, who attempted to bar his way, with detached corps under Joubert and Masséna. Bonaparte was irresistible. He forced his way to within a short distance of Vienna, and finally at Leoben, on the 18th of April, Austria accepted peace preliminaries. She agreed to cede the Netherlands and Lombardy, in return for which she was to receive certain compensations.

Bonaparte was now negotiator as well as general. For the Directoire was in great danger; it had come face to face with a situation in which it required all the support its general could give, and in return conceded to him a corresponding increase of powers. In March and April the first election for the renewal of the Councils was held, and out of 216 outgoing ex-conventionnels who appealed to the electorate, 205 were defeated at the polls. A more unanimous pronouncement of public opinion was hardly possible.

But the Directors were not capable of accepting the verdict of the country; power was theirs, and they were resolved it should remain theirs. In the Councils an extreme party led by Boissy d' Anglas, Pichegru and Camille Jordan, embarked on a policy of turning out the Directors and repealing all the revolutionary legislation, especially that directed against the *émigrés* and the Church. They formed the Club de Clichy. In the centre of the house opinions were more moderate,—moderate progressive, and moderate Jacobin; in the latter party, Sieyès, Talleyrand, Benjamin Constant, and as a social and literary influence, the daughter of Necker, Mme. de Staël.

The first step in the struggle was marked by the election of Barthélemy, the negotiator of the treaty of Bale and a moderate, to the Directoire instead of Letourneur, who retired by rotation. Long debates followed on the *émigrés* and the priests, and their course led to an attack by the Councils, supported by Carnot and Barthélemy, on the Ministry. Some changes were made, and it was at this moment that Talleyrand secured the post of Minister of Foreign Affairs.

The Five Hundred now became interested in some rather obscure negotiations that Bonaparte was conducting in Italy with a view to converting the peace preliminaries of Leoben into a definite treaty. No sooner had he disposed of Austria than he had treacherously turned on Venice and seized the city. He was now juggling with this and the other French acquisitions in Italy in rather dubious fashion, and the orators of the opposition fastened on this as a text. It was just at this moment that Barras turned to his old protégé and asked for his help. Bonaparte's sword leapt from the scabbard instantly. He issued a proclamation to his army denouncing the factious opposition of the Clichiens; and he sent Augereau, his grenadier general, to Barras' assistance. The result was the revolution of Fructidor.

Late on the 3rd of September, Barras, Rewbell and Larevellière, announced the discovery of a great royalist conspiracy. Barthélemy was arrested; Carnot just succeeded in escaping. Next morning Augereau with 2,000 men surrounded the assembly, arrested Pichegru and several leading members, and prevented the other members from meeting. Meanwhile small groups of supporters of Barras from the two Councils came together and proceeded to transact business. On the 5th, the 19th of Fructidor, decrees were passed by the usurping bodies; they provided for the deportation of Carnot, Barthélemy, Pichegru and others; they arbitrarily annulled a number of elections; they ordered all returned *émigrés* to leave France; they repealed a recent law in favour of liberty of worship, and they placed the press under strict Government control. On the next day two new Directors were chosen from the successful faction, Merlin de Douai and François de Neufchateau.

The Fructidorians now controlled the situation, led by Tallien, Chénier, Jourdan in the Councils. Many officials were removed and replaced by their adherents. Priests were severely repressed, thousands being imprisoned. Military tribunals were formed to deal with *émigrés,* and, in the course of the next two years, sent nearly 200 to the firing party.

Six weeks after Fructidor, on the 17th of October, the long struggle between France and Austria was concluded by the treaty of Campo Formio, signed by Bonaparte and Cobenzl. Austria ceded the Netherlands to France; her Lombard province was incorporated in the newly formed Cisalpine Republic, which she recognised; all the left bank of the Rhine from Bale was ceded to France; Austria took Venice; and a congress was to meet at Rastatt to consider territorial readjustments within the Empire.

After Fructidor and Campo Formio matters proceeded more quietly for awhile, the close of the year being marked by only two incidents that need be recorded here, one the departure of Sieyès as ambassador to Berlin, the other the triumphant return of Bonaparte from Italy, and the ovations which the Parisian public gave him. But meanwhile, even with the Councils packed, the Directors were once more in difficulties, for the financial situation was getting worse and worse, and the venality, extravagance and incapacity of the Government seemed likely to result in a general bankruptcy. Already 145,000,000,000,000 of assignats had been issued. Gold was difficult to procure, a quotation for a louis in 1797 being three thousand and eighty francs in paper. A new form of assignat had been tried, but without much success. The expenses of the war were enormous, an army of over 1,000,000 men having doubled the annual expenses of the State. Had not Bonaparte systematically bled Italy of money and treasure the Directoire could not have conducted business so long. As it was, it could go on no longer. The new taxes, on property and income, had not become effective, largely because collection was devolved on the communes. And so, a few days after the revolution of Fructidor, a partial bankruptcy was declared; interest payments were suspended on two-thirds of the debt.

In the following spring, March-April 1798, the elections once more proved disastrous to the Directors. They really had few supporters beyond those who held office under them, or who hoped for their turn to come to hold office. Over 400 deputies were to be chosen, and opinion was still so hostile that the only chance of the Directors was in illegal action. They tampered with the elections; and, finding this insufficient to accomplish their object, succeeded by another stroke of violence in getting a decree, on the 4th of May, 22d of Floréal, excluding a number of the newly elected deputies. All this proved in vain. The temper of the Councils was solidly hostile, and now the hostility came as much from the Jacobin as from any other part of the house.

Partly from weakness, partly to create a diversion, the Directoire was now drifting into a new war. In February, owing to French intrigues, a riot took place at Rome, which resulted in a republic being proclaimed and the Pope being driven from the city. Further north the same process was repeated. French troops occupied Bern, and under their influence an Helvetic republic came into existence. Meanwhile, the war with England continued with increased vigour; a great stroke was aimed at England's colonial empire of the East, Bonaparte sailing from Toulon for Egypt on the 19th of May. On the 12th of June he seized Malta; on the 21st of July he routed the Mamelukes in the battle of the Pyramids; and on the 1st of August his fleet was destroyed at its anchorage, near the mouth of the Nile, by Admiral Nelson. The best army and the best general of the Directoire were cut off in Egypt.

Meanwhile Nelson, returning to Italy to refit his ships, decided the court of Naples to join in the war against France, and determined the march of Ferdinand and his army against Rome, which city he occupied on the 29th of November. Championnet, commander of the French forces in southern Italy, brought one more flash of triumph to his country's arms; though heavily outnumbered, he drove Ferdinand out of Rome, followed him to Naples, and took the city by storm after desperate street fighting at the end of December.

At Naples, as elsewhere, France set up a vassal state, the Parthenopean Republic, that lived but few weeks and ended in tragedy. For early in the year 1799, Austria and Russia placed an army in the field in northern Italy, the war with Austria beginning in March. Its first events took place in Germany, where Jourdan, for the fourth time attempting to force his way through the valley of the Danube, once more met with failure. The Archduke Charles fought him at Stockach, and there defeated him. This defeat gave the northern command to Masséna and sent Jourdan back to politics. When, some years later, the victor of Fleurus was again entrusted with the command of large armies, it was only to lead them to failure at Talavera, and to disaster at Vittoria.

Just as the war with Austria broke out again, the yearly elections for the Councils were being held. The war brought about a recurrence of revolutionary fever, which resulted in great Jacobin successes at the polls. But the new deputies, like the old, were hostile to the discredited Directoire. France wanted some stronger, abler, more honest, more dignified executive than she had; she would no longer tolerate that a gang of shady politicians should fatten in an office they did nothing to make effective. And as the war cloud grew blacker and the national finances more exhausted, the Jacobins themselves undertook to reform the Republic. The first step was to get a strong foothold in the enemy's camp. This was effected by electing Sieyès to fill the vacancy caused by the retirement of Rewbell from the Directoire,—Sieyès, who was known for his hostility to the existing system, whose reputation for solidity and political integrity was wide, whose capacity as a constitutionalist and reformer was extraordinarily overrated.

With Sieyès on the Directoire there comes into existence an ill-defined, vague conspiracy, all the more dangerous in that it was far more a general push of a great number of men towards a new set of conditions, than a cut-and-dried plot involving precise action and precise results at a given moment.. In this new set of conditions Sieyès, and those who thought with him, recognised one fact as inevitable, the fact Robespierre had so early foreseen and so constantly dreaded. The influence of the army must be brought in; and the influence of the army meant the influence of one of the generals. And as Sieyès and his friends looked about for a general to suit their purpose, they found it difficult to pick their man. Bonaparte had long been cut off in Egypt by the English fleet, and news of his army only reached Paris after long delays and at long intervals. Jourdan had almost lost his prestige by his continued ill success, and was in any case indisposed to act with Sieyès. In Italy all the generals were doing badly.

The Russian field marshal Suvaroff, with an Austro-Russian army, was sweeping everything before him. On the 27th of April he defeated Moreau at Cassano; he then occupied Milan, and drove the French south into Genoa.

At this moment Macdonald, who had succeeded Championnet at Naples, was marching northwards to join Moreau. Suvaroff got between them and, after three days' hard fighting, from the 17th to the 19th of June, inflicted a second severe defeat on the French, at La Trebbia. These reverses shattered the whole French domination of Italy; their armies were defeated, their vassal republics sank, that of Naples under horrible conditions of royalist reprisal and massacre.

The Directoire suffered heavily in prestige by the events of a war which it had so lightly provoked and was so incompetent to conduct. In June the Councils made a further successful attack on the Executive and succeeded, in quick succession, in forcing out three of the Directors, Treilhard, Larevellière, and Merlin. For them were substituted Gohier, who was colourless; Moulin, who was stupid, and Ducos, who was pliable. Of the Thermidorians Barras alone remained, and Barras, after five years of uninterrupted power and luxury, was used up as a man of action; he was quite ready to come to reasonable terms with Sieyès, or, if matters should turn that way, with the Comte de Provence, whose agents were in touch with him.

Sieyès who owed his position in great part to the support of the Jacobins in the Council of Five Hundred, now found them an obstacle. The defeats of the armies were making them unruly. They had formed a club, meeting in the *Manège,* that threatened to develop all the characteristics of the old Jacobin Club, and that caused widespread alarm. The Ancients ordered the closing of the *Manège*. But the Jacobins, led by Jourdan, Bernadotte, minister of war, and others, continued their meetings in new quarters. They began to clamour for a new committee of public safety.

Sieyès now selected Joubert to retrieve the situation. This young general had been one of Bonaparte's most brilliant divisional commanders. He had a strong following in the army, was a staunch republican, and was possibly a general of the first order. He was sent for, was told to assume command in Italy, and was given every battalion that could possibly be scraped together. With these he was to win a battle decisive not only of the fate of Italy but of that of the Republic and of the Directoire.

Joubert left Paris on the 16th of July. A month later, having concentrated all that was left of the Italian armies together with his reinforcements at Genoa, he marched north. At Novi, half way to the Po, Suvaroff barred his advance. A great battle was fought; the French were heavily defeated; and Joubert was killed. One week later, just as the disastrous news of Novi was reaching Paris, General Bonaparte with a few officers of his staff embarked at Alexandria, and risking the English men of war, set sail for France.

Bonaparte now becomes the central figure on the historical stage, and the events that follow belong to his history more than to that of the Revolution. Here all that remains to be done is to indicate the nature of the change that now took place, his connection with the schemes of Sieyès for ridding France of the Directoire and placing something more effective in its stead.

While Bonaparte was sailing the Mediterranean,—seven long weeks from Alexandria to Fréjus,—the disgust and weariness of France increased. Jourdan and Bernadotte, in a blundering way, attempted to wrest power from the Directors, but proved unequal in prestige and ability to the task;—a more powerful and more subtle political craftsman was needed. Then in the gloom of the public despondence three sudden flashes electrified the air, flash on flash. Masséna, with the last army of the Republic, turning sharply right and left, beat the Austrians, destroyed Suvaroff in the mountains of Switzerland about Zurich. Before the excitement had subsided, came a despatch from the depths of the Mediterranean, penned with Ossianic exaggeration by the greatest of political romanticists, in which was announced the destruction of a turbaned army of Turks at Aboukir by the irresistible demi-brigades of the old army of Italy. And then, suddenly, people ran out into the streets to be told that the man himself was in France; Bonaparte had landed at Fréjus.

Rarely has a country turned to an individual as France turned to Bonaparte at that moment. And he, playing with cool mastery and well-contained judgment on the political instrument fate had placed in his hands, announced himself as the man of peace, of reform, of strong civil government, of republican virtue. It was one long ovation from Fréjus to Paris.

At Paris Bonaparte judged, and judged rightly, that the pear, as he crudely put it, was ripe. All parties came to him, and Sieyès came to him. The author of that epoch-making pamphlet *Qu 'estce que le Tiers Etat?*, and the greatest soldier produced by the Revolution, put their heads together to bring the Revolution to an end.

Sieyès and Bonaparte effected their purpose on the 9th and 10th of November, the 18th and 19th of Brumaire. The method they adopted was merely a slight development of that used by Barras and Augereau at the Revolution of Fructidor two years earlier. Some of the Directors were put under constraint; others supported the conspiracy. But the Council of Five Hundred resisted strenuously, and it was only after scenes of great violence that it succumbed. It was only at the tap of the army drums and at the flash of serried bayonets, that the last assembly of the Revolution abandoned its post. The man of the sword, so long foreseen and dreaded by Robespierre, had come into his own, and the Republic had made way for the Consulate.

CHAPTER XVII

ART AND LITERATURE

FRENCH literature has great names before 1789, and after 1815. Voltaire, Diderot, Rousseau, to mention only the giants, wrote before the Revolution; and, Chateaubriand, Thiers, Hugo, Musset, Béranger, Courrier, after Napoleon had fallen. In between there is little or nothing. The period is like a desolate site devastated by flame, stained with blood, with only here and there a timid flower lending a little colour, a touch of grace, a gleam of beauty, to a scene of destruction and violence.

No verse or prose of the period gives the note of the Revolution on its idealistic side more strikingly than Fabre d' Eglantine's nomenclature of the months for the Revolutionary Calendar. Although slightly tinged with pedantism and preciosity, its freshness, its grace, its inspiration and sincerity, give it a flavour almost of primitive art. It remains one of the few notable prose poems of French literature.

VENDÉMIAIRE,
premier mois de l'année rèpublicaine et de l'automne;
prend son étymologie des vendanges
qui ont lieu pendant ce mois.

BRUMAIRE,
deuxième mois de l'année républicaine;
il tire son nom des brouillards et des brumes basses
qui font en quelque sorte la transsudation de la nature pendant ce mois.

FRIMAIRE,
troisième mois de l'année républicaine,
ainsi nommé du froid tantôt sec, tantôt humide,
qui se fait sentit pendant ce mois.

NIVÔSE,
quatrième mois de l'année républicaine, et le premier de l'hiver;
il prend son étymologie de la neige
qui blanchit la terre pendant ce mois.

PLUVIÔSE,
cinquième mois de l'année républicaine;
il tire son nom des pluies
qui tombent généralement avec plus d'abondance pendant ce mois.

VENTÔSE,
sixième mois de l'année républicaine,
ainsi nommé des giboulées qui ont lieu, et du vent
qui vient sécher la terre pendant ce mois.

Germinal,
septième mois de l'année républicaine, et le premier du printemps;
il prend son étymologie
de la fermentation et du développement de la sève pendant ce mois.

Floréal,
huitième mois de l'année républicaine,
ainsi nommé de l'épanouissement des fleurs
que la terre produit pendant ce mois.

Prairial,
neuvième mois de l'année républicaine;
il tire son nom de la fécondité riante
et de la récolte des prairies pendant ce mois.

Messidor,
dixième mois de l'année républicaine, et le premier de l'été;
il prend son étymologie de l'aspect des épis ondoyans et des moissons dorées
qui couvrent les champs pendant ce mois.

Thermidor,
onzième mois de l'année républicaine,
ainsi nommé de la chaleur tout-à-la-fois solaire et terrestre
qui embrase l'air pendant ce mois.

Fructidor,
douzième mois de l'année républicaine;
il tire son nom des fruits
que le soleil dore et mûrit pendant ce mois.[1]

---

[1] TO THE NUMBER OF THE DAY IN:
Vendémiare, add 21 to get dates in September, October;

Fabre d' Eglantine was not the only member of the assemblies of the Revolution to deserve a place in literature. The great orators, Mirabeau, Danton, Vergniaud, Robespierre, and others, rose to a high pitch of rhetoric in their speeches. Famous apostrophes which they uttered are still current phrases: Nous sommes .ici par le volonté du peuple, et nous n' ont sortirout que par le force des bayonettes. —Silence aux trente voix!—De l' audace, encore de l' audace, et toujours de l' audace! Some extracts from the orators have been given in preceding chapters, and the pamphleteers have also been drawn from; the latter, even in the pages of Desmoulins, Loustallot or Mallet, rarely attain the level of the best literature.

Brumaire, add 21 to get dates in October, November;
Frimaire, add 20 to get dates in November, December;
Nivôse, add 20 to get dates in December, January;
Pluviose, add 19 to get dates in January, February;
Ventôse, add 18 to get dates in February, March;
Germinal, add 20 to get dates in March, April;
Floréal, add 19 to get dates in April, May;
Prairial, add 19 to get dates in May, June;
Messidor, add 18 to get dates in June, July;
Thermidor, add 18 to get dates in July, August;
Fructidor, add 17 to get dates in August, September;
Fructidor was followed by five *jours supplémentaires,* the *sans cullotides.*

The following passage from Desmoulins shows the unfortunate journalist at his best, when, backed by Danton, in December 1793, he raised the standard of mercy against terrorism and the infamous sans-culottism of Hébert.

> O mes chers concitoyens! Serions nous donc arrivés à ce point que de nous prosterner devant de telles divinités? Non, la Liberté, cette Liberté descendue du ciel, ce n'est point une nymphe de l'Opéra, ce n'est point un bonnet rouge, une chemise sale, ou des haillons. La Liberté, c'est le bonheur, c'est la raison, c'est l'égalité, c'est la justice. . . . Voulez vous que je la reconnaisse, que je tombe a ses pieds, que je verse tout mon sang pour elle? ouvrez les prisons. . . .

Few poets marked the epoch, and of their works the most famous are battle songs. Rouget de Lisle, on the declaration of war against Austria in April 1792, composed the music and words of the best known song in the world, the famous Marseillaise. One of its strophes follows:

> Amour sacré de la patrie,
> Conduis, soutiens, nos bras vengeurs.
> Liberté, liberté chérie,
> Combats avec tes défenseurs.

Sous nos drapeaux que la victoire
Accoure à tes mâles accens,
Que tes enemis expirans
Voient ton triomphe et notre gloire.
Aux armes, citoyens! Formez vos bataillons!
Marchez; qu'un sang impur abreuve nos sillons.

A better song poem than the *Marseillaise,* though not quite so famous, was written by Joseph Chénier, the *Chant du départ;* it was a great favourite with Bonaparte.

La victoire, en chantant, nous ouvre la barrière,
La liberté guide nos pas,
Et du nord au midi, la trompette guerrière
A sonné l'heure des combats;
Tremblez enemis de la France,
Rois ivres de sang et d'orgueil,
Le peuple souverain s'avance;
Tyrans, descendez au cercueil!
La République nous appelle,
Sachons vaincre ou sachons périr,
Un Français doit vivre pour elle,
Pour elle, un Français doit mourir!

With the Chéniers we come to the one considerable poet of the revolutionary period, André, brother of the author of the *Chant du départ*. He was sent to the guillotine on the

7th of Thermidor at the age of 31, having published only two poems, one on the Oath of the tennis court in 1789, and the other on the festival organized for the Swiss of Chateauvieux' mutinous regiment by Collot d' Herbois in the spring of 1792. The opening lines of his first poem strike the note of a new era:

Reprends ta robe d'or, ceins ton riche bandeau,
Jeune et divine poésie,
Quoique ces temps d'orage eclipsent ton flambeau.
. . . .
La liberté du génie et de l'art
T'ouvre tous les trésors. Ta grâce auguste et fière
De nature et d'éternité
Fleurit. Tes pas sont grands. Ton front ceint de lumière
Touche les cieux. . . .

And foreseeing, as a poet should, the tragedies to come, he pleads for guidance to avert the resulting woes from the people:

Ah, ne le laissez pas, dans la sanglante rage
D' un ressentiment inhumain,
Souiller sa cause et votre ouvrage.
Ah! ne le laissez pas sans conseil et sans frein,
Armant, pour soutenir ses droits si légitimes,
La torche incendiaire et le fer assassin,
Venger la raison par des crimes.

Always among the moderates, Chénier was revolted by the apotheosis accorded by Collot and the democratic party to the Swiss of the regiment of Chateauvieux. On the 15th of April 1792 he published some stinging verses on the subject, that possibly cost him his life.

Salut, divin triomphe! entre dans nos murailles;
  Rend nous ces guerriers illustrés
Par le sang de Désille et par les funérailles
  De tant de Français massacrés. . . .
Un seul jour peut atteindre à tant de renommée,
  Et ce beau jour luira bientôt:
C'est quand tu conduiras Jourdan à notre armée,
  Et Lafayette à l'échafaud. . . .
Invoque en leur galère, ornement des étoiles,
  Les Suisses de Collot d'Herbois. . . .
Ces héros que jadis sur les bancs des galères
  Assit un arrêt outrageant,
Et qui n'ont égorgé que très peu de nos frères
  Et volé que très peu d'argent!

Among the verses published after Chénier's death the most striking are those that have to deal with the period of the reign of terror; of these a few lines will be quoted. The poet raised his voice while all Paris howled against Charlotte Corday, the assassin of Marat:

Non, non, je ne veux point honorer en silence,
Toi qui crus par ta mort resusciter la France
Et dévouas tes jours à punir des forfaits.
Le glaive arma ton bras, fille grande et sublime,
Pour faire honte aux dieux, pour réparer leur crime,
Quand d'un homme à ce monstre ils donnèrent les
traits.

Mais la France à la hache abandonne ta tête,
C'est au monstre égorgé qu'on prépare une fête.
Parmi ses compagnons, tous dignes de son sort,
Oh! quel noble dédain fit sourire ta bouche,
Quand un brigand, vengeur de ce brigand farouche,
Crut te faire pâlir aux menaces de mort!

C'est lui qui dut pâlir, et tes juges sinistres,
Et notre affreux sénat, et ses affreux ministres,
Quand, à leur tribunal, sans crainte et sans appui,
Ta douceur, ton langage et simple et magnanime
Leur apprit qu'en effet, tout puissant qu'est le crime,
Qui renonce à la vie est plus puissant que lui.

Carrier and the atrocities at Nantes gave him an even stronger text:

Vingt barques, faux tissus de planches fugitives,
S'entrouvrant au milieu des eaux,
Ont elles, par milliers, dans les gouffres de Loire
Vomi des Français enchainés,
Au proconsul Carrier, implacable après boire,

Pour son passetemps amenés?
Et ces porte-plumets, ces commis de carnage,
Ces noirs accusateurs Fouquiers,
Ces Dumas, ces jurés, horrible aréopage
De voleurs et de meurtriers,
Les ai-je poursuivis jusqu'en leurs bacchanales,
Lorsque, les yeux encore ardents,
Attablés, le bordeaux de chaleurs brutales
Allumant leurs fronts impudents,
Ivres et bégayant la crapule et les crimes,
Ils rappellent avec des ris,
Leurs meurtres d'aujourd'hui, leurs futures victimes,
Et parmi les chansons, les cris,
Trouvent deça, dela, sous leur main, sous leur bouche,
De femmes un vénal essaim,
Dépouilles du vaincu, transfuges de sa couche,
Pour la couche de l'assassin?

The writer of such lines could not hope to escape the proscriptions of the Terror; and it was in prison, awaiting his turn for the guillotine, that his last fragments were written. There a young girl, a fellow prisoner, became the heroine of perhaps his most beautiful lines:

LA JEUNE CAPTIVE.

"L'epi naissant mûrit, de la faux respecté;
Sans crainte du pressoir, le pampre tout l'été
Boit les doux présents de l'aurore;
Et moi, comme lui belle, et jeune comme lui,

Quoique l'heure présente ait de trouble et d'ennui,
Je ne veux point mourir encore.

"Je ne suis qu'au printemps, je veux voir la moisson;
Et comme le soleil, de saison en saison,
Je veux achever mon année.
Brillante sur ma tige, et l'honneur du jardin,
Je n'ai vu luire encore que les feux du matin,
Je veux achever ma journée.

. . . .

Ainsi, triste et captif, ma lyre toutefois
S'éveillait, écoutant ces plaintes, cette voix,
Ces vœux d'une jeune captive;
Et secouant le faix de mes jours languissants,
Aux douces lois des vers je pliais les accents
De sa bouche aimable et naïve.

One last quotation gives a picture of the prison of St. Lazare, whence he went to the scaffold a few days after penning these lines:

Ici même, en ces parcs ou la mort nous fait paitre,
Ou la hache nous tire au sort,
Beaux poulets sont écrits; maris, amants sont dupes.
Caquetages; intrigues de sots.
On y chante, on y joue, on y lève des jupes;
On y fait chansons et bon mots;
L'un pousse et fait bondir sur les toits, sur les vitres,
Un ballon tout gonflé de vent,
Comme sont les discours des sept cents plats bélîtres,

Dont Barère est le plus savant.
L'autre court ; l'autre saute ; et braillent, boivent, rient,
Politiqueurs et raisonneurs ;
Et sur les gonds de fer soudain les portes crient,
Des juges tigres nos seigneurs
Le pourvoyeur parait. Quelle sera la proie
Que la hache appelle aujourd'hui ?

François de Neufchateau, who became a Director after the revolution of Fructidor, and the younger Chénier, were perhaps the best dramatists of the epoch. The former hardly deserves extended notice. Chénier's *Charles IX,* played at the outbreak of the Revolution, had a great success as a political play, and he followed it up with several others that served as pegs on which excited audiences might hang their political hats. Voltaire's *Brutus,* unplayable half a century before, was all the vogue now; and the dramatist had only to air democratic sentiments to please his audience.

The thing went far, and art suffered in the process. Plot and dialogue took on the feverish colours of the Revolution. Audiences howled *la Carmagnole* or the *ça ira,* before the curtain went up; and when the play began, revelled in highly-spiced, political dramatics, in which the Pope soon became the most reviled and popular of villains. The Pope drunk, the Pope kicked in the stomach by his brutal confederate George III, the Pope making love to Madame de Polignac, the Pope sursounded by the tyrants of Europe swallowed up by the flame-belching volcano of an enchanted island, such were the titbits that brought moisture to the palates of the connoisseurs of the drama in Paris.

The efforts of Joseph Chénier to get his tragedy *Timoléon,* played, at a moment when he was not in good repute with the Committee of Public Safety, may serve as an example of many similar incidents. The words, "We need laws, not blood," in his *Charles IX,* had displeased Robespierre and Billaud-Varennes, and the Jacobins were resolved to prevent any new production. He read the Ms. of his *Timoléon* however, with great success, to the company of the Théatre de la République. Vilate may be left to continue the tale:

Le lendemain je me trouve placé, dans la Société des Jacobins, prés David et Michot. Celui-ci disait à l'autre: *Ah! la belle tragédie que celle de Timoléon; c'est un chef d'œuvre; demande a Vilate.* Je ne pus me défendre de rendre une justice éclatante . . . au génie de l'auteur. Le peintre (David) . . . nous répond: *Chénier une belle tragédie! c'est impossible. Son âme a-t-elle jamais pu sentir la liberté pour la bien rendre? Non, je n'y crois pas.* A quelques jours de là, me trouvant avec Barère et Billaud-Varennes, on parle de *Timoléon.* Billaud ne put dissimuler son humeur: *Elle ne vaut rien; elle n'aura pas l'honneur de la représentation. Qu'entend-il par ce vers contre-révolutionaire:*

N'est on jamais tyran qu'avec un diadème?

Barère, qui avait mêlé ses applaudissements à la lecture de la pièce, mais auquel j'avais déja rapporté les propos de. David, ajoute: *Oui, il n'y a pas de génie révolutionaire; elle manque dans le plan.* Billaud à Barère: *Ne souffrons pas qu'elle soit jouée.* Barère: *Donnons lui le plaisir de quelques répétitions.*

Several rehearsals were accordingly permitted to take place. Two performances followed. At the third there came a collapse.

Ou laisse aller la tragédie jusqu' à la scène on Aristocles va pour placer le bandeau royal sur la tête de Timophane, sous prétexte que le peuple de Corinthe concentre son indignation. . . .

A man in the pit thereupon rose and called out:

Si le peuple eut besoin d' être provoqué pour s' élever contre la tyrannie, c'est une injure faite au peuple français que de lui offrir cet exemple de faiblesse et d' ineptie. A bas la toile!

The cry was taken up; a riotous scene followed; and presently: on pousse l' horreur jusqu' au point de forcer Chénier â bruler lui-même, sur le théatre, le fruit de huit mois de travaux et de veilles.

Art, like literature, languished during the Revolution, or meretriciously touched herself up with the fashionable rouge. Before and after are great periods, but for the moment art seems to have lost its cunning; the artist, like David, turns politician. Fragonard and Greuze both survived to see the Empire, but lost their vogue. The touch of Greuze could hardly be appreciated in the age of Danton; the luscious sweetness of Fragonard was in like case; both of these great artists were ruined by the Revolution and died in poverty. Instead of these graceful masters of the false pastoral taste of the decaying century, a robust group of military painters arises, Vernet, Charlet, Géricault, and later Raffet, most brutal, but most candid portrayer of the armies of the Republic. The false classical style, inherited from the period of Louis XVI, is metamorphosed by David and Gros, becomes inflated, declamatory, vapid, and wooden. David's immense picture, the most insistent canvas now hanging in the Louvre, representing the three Horatii swearing to Rome that they would conquer or die, gives the note of the period. False sentiment, mock heroics, glittering formula, lay figure attitude, all are there.

A few artists succeeded in carrying the elegance of the 18th century through the storm into the period beyond, notably Prud'hon, who has been called the Watteau of the Revolution. His portraits of the women of the Bonaparte family, Joséphine, Hortense, Pauline, have all the grace and fascination of the earlier age, merge with it the abandon of the Directoire period, and touch the whole with the romanticism and individualism of the coming century. In terrible contrast with these lovely and alluring women of the new age, is the grim figure caught in a few masterly strokes by David, as Marie Antoinette, proud and unbending as ever, but shorn of all the glory of Versailles, her face haggard, her hair gray, dishevelled, mutilated by scissors, passed by on the prisoner's cart on her way to the guillotine. It is the guillotine, in art as in politics the most potent of solvents, that stands between Trianon and the romantics.

END

INDEX

OF NAMES OF PLACES AND PERSONS